"David Leach does an admirable job defending liberty against the multitude of threats that seek to extinguish it."

—DR. RON PAUL,

Twelve-term U.S. congressman and former presidential candidate

"True liberty is endangered, and our country and America's future are imperiled as constitutional rights are twisted and denied by both parties. Politicians from both sides pick and choose the framing that fits their own agendas. In David Leach's book, *The New Axis of Evil: Exposing the Bipartisan War on Liberty*, he unpacks how politicians are threatening our conservative Christian values and the foundation that our Christ-honoring forefathers fought for. An illuminating and insightful must-read for anyone who loves and is willing to stand strong for our nation's future!"

—MIKE TRIEM,

Crawford Media Group General Manager
KLTT/KLZ/KLDC/KLVZ - Denver

THE NEW AXIS OF EVIL

Exposing the Bipartisan War on Liberty

DAVID LEACH

S C
PRESS

To my wife, Jeanne. I wouldn't be the man I am without you. I love you big as the sky!

TABLE OF CONTENTS

FOREWORD

What does "liberty" mean to you and me? I've often found myself thinking about this question, particularly over the past few years, and here's what I've come up with.

Liberty means possessing the freedom to live outside what the elitists in government tell us about what this world should be. Liberty means we are free to meet God and to be what He means for us to be.

To live in liberty is to connect with our spiritual roots and make them physical, thus allowing us to live a life not dictated by fads, trends, or worldly pursuits; to walk in the profound and eternal truth that we are fearfully and wonderfully made by a Creator who loves us.

We are individuals. We are *more* than "the collective." We are more than an abstract "global community." We are *independent*!

We have been equipped by *the* sovereign, powerful, and almighty God to care for ourselves, our families, and our local communities. We don't need planners or owners or an overbearing and out-of-control government to take care of us. All we need is our faith in God and a commitment to this ultimate truth: that we have been endowed by Him with the unalienable rights to life, liberty, and the pursuit of happiness.

Living in liberty means we can cherish and respect those who disagree with us and pursue a lifestyle different from ours. And we can tolerate those who hate us for our Christian beliefs, our conservative values, and our uncompromising commitment to the Constitution. Though we disagree, we afford these people the same liberty that God afforded all mankind: the *choice* to accept Him and His grace or to reject Him.

Living in liberty means we willingly accept the consequences of our choices and actions, and we take responsibility for our failures and our successes. We understand that living in liberty comes with many dangers and risks, but they are less dangerous than the risk of sacrificing our self-sufficiency and our families to the whims of an entitled collective.

As Thomas Jefferson once said, "I would rather be exposed to the inconveniences attending too much liberty than to those attending too small a degree of it."

Liberty is the ultimate peacemaker because it allows each person, each family, and each town or village to pursue their own happiness.

Over my many years as a dedicated Christian, business owner, and community organizer, I've developed a passion for liberty and genuine discourse, and that has led me to other like-minded, liberty lovers who understand the times we are living in. David Leach is one of those people.

As a co-warrior and friend, I have come to appreciate David's ability to expose the enemies of liberty regardless of party labels and biased agendas. His Christian faith, his conservative values, and his commitment to the Constitution serve as a reminder that we need to have the courage and conviction to stand up for what is right, even when it's unpopular to do so.

The New Axis of Evil: Exposing the Bipartisan War on Liberty is a must-read for anyone who's tired of seeing liberty systematically dismantled by self-interested politicians, their allies in the media, and religious leaders who have become all too willing to trade God for political power.

Shannon Joy is the host of The Shannon Joy Show, a program dedicated to fearless cultural and political commentary that cuts through the noise of the mainstream media. Find her at theshannonjoy.com

AMERICA IN TRAUMA

"An unacknowledged trauma is like a wound that never heals over and may start to bleed again at any time."[1]

ALICE MILLER,

Ph.D. in philosophy, psychology, and sociology

CHAPTER 1

SEEING WITH CLARITY

"What lies behind us and what lies before us are tiny matters compared to what lies within us."[2]

RALPH WALDO EMERSON
(American philosopher, abolitionist, and poet)

"Freedom is never more than one generation away from extinction. We didn't pass it to our children in the bloodstream. It must be fought for, protected, and handed on for them to do the same."[3]

RONALD REAGAN
(40th president of the United States)

"Beyond the fog lies clarity."

ANONYMOUS

Nothing is more crucial to the human experience than liberty. And yet it is perhaps the one thing about which we are least clear.

America's journey has been a road filled with the unexpected. The Founding Fathers may have set out to create a nation where We the People could "secure the blessings of Liberty to ourselves and our posterity," but the reality is that the road has been filled with potholes and detours.

Where is the promise of our God-given rights to life, liberty, and the pursuit of happiness?

Where is the Bill of Rights when we need it most?

What is to become of our great Republic?

Just as wind and water gradually carved the Grand Canyon, the cumulative effect of decades of not really understanding the answers to these questions has led to a subtle, persistent erosion where we doubt the reason for our existence, the goodness of America, and the things that make us good.

Over time, this has led us to forget that our rights come from God and that liberty is essential to our existence. And with no understanding of these fundamental truths, we have reached a point where we delegate power to the government it was never supposed to have.

But knowing this means nothing if we're unaware of what liberty looks like or what we need to do to find it and live in it again.

According to the *Farmers' Almanac*[4] and the *World Atlas*[5], the foggiest place in the world is the Grand Banks, a spot off the island of Newfoundland, Canada, where the chilly Labrador Current from the north meets up with the much warmer Gulf Stream from the south, creating 206 foggy days per year. Because fog reduces visibility, it's difficult for people to see through it to know where they are and where they're going.

When it comes to liberty in America, doesn't it seem we're that way 365 days a year? Where did we miss the mark, and how did we miss it so badly? How did we end up where we are today? Where do we go from here?

Today, in an almost desperate attempt to salvage what we can of the American Dream, we vote for politicians representing "our side" who promise to do the things necessary to "secure the blessings of liberty to ourselves and our posterity," as mentioned in the preamble of the Constitution.

Still, we usually end up with more of the same ol' same ol'. And even when those politicians appear to make a little progress, it almost always comes with an unintended consequence of some sort—usually a loss of a little bit of our freedom. Sure, Republicans and Democrats talk about how their agendas won't interfere with our right to live in liberty, but we typically see very little evidence that this is true.

How can a nation that claims to believe, as Benjamin Franklin once said, that "Freedom is not a gift bestowed upon us by other men, but a right that belongs to us by the laws of God and nature" continue to exist under such dysfunction? When stood side by side, liberty in America today is a far cry from the liberty our Founding Fathers fought and died for.

Perhaps the reason for our current condition is that we've been trapped in the fog for so long that we have become disoriented and, in the process, disconnected from our heart—our heart of liberty.

The consequences of this disorientation and disconnection are clear. Fundamental liberties such as freedom of speech, freedom of religion, and freedom of the press are routinely sacrificed on the altar of political agendas.

MISINFORMATION OR FREE SPEECH

Republicans and Democrats in Washington have taken to redefining free speech as misinformation or disinformation—which is political doublespeak used to describe people exercising their First Amendment free speech right to say things the government doesn't approve of—and criminalizing it. We see this happening in several areas today.

THE LGBT AGENDA AND RELIGIOUS LIBERTY

The assault on religious liberty is multifaceted, but the LGBT agenda and the sexual tyranny it has created have become the most severe threat to this First Amendment right. No longer the stuff of "whatever goes on behind closed doors is nobody's business," the culture war against morality and the constitutionally protected Freedom of Religion that is being waged by LGBT extremists and their allies in Washington has been steadily working to destroy this God-given right.

FAKE NEWS OR FREEDOM OF THE PRESS

From Franklin Delano Roosevelt to Joe Biden, Republican and Democrat presidents alike have tried to silence the media in all its forms (print, radio, television, internet) for reporting unfavorably on their policies, when they break a promise, or get caught in a lie.

Just like falling dominoes, the denial of our First Amendment rights has led to the fall of most of the Bill of Rights, such as:

► **The right of the people to keep and bear arms (Second Amendment)** The assault on the right to own firearms has been part of the Republican/ Democrat agenda going back to Richard Nixon, who pushed for a national ban on handguns because "guns are an abomination."[6] Recent history is full of examples of the government's attempt to void the Second Amendment.

► **The right of the people to be secure in their persons, houses, papers, and effects against unreasonable searches and seizures (Fourth Amendment)** This is another area where red flag laws violate the Constitution. Additionally, the growth of the government's surveillance powers has created an environment where people are no longer safe from unreasonable searches and seizures.

▶ **The right of the people not to be deprived of life, liberty, or property without due process of law (Fifth Amendment)** Red flag laws, government spying, and government mandates—all these and more deprive us of our right to due process.

▶ **The right of the people to limit the power of the federal government through the states (Tenth Amendment)** The Tenth Amendment clearly and plainly states, "The powers not delegated to the United States by the Constitution, nor prohibited by it to the states, are reserved to the states respectively, or to the people." Still, Washington routinely overrides the power of the states in the name of Washington's agenda.

The disconnect from our heart of liberty has led, and continues to lead, to the gradual erosion of these God-given rights.

In today's political and spiritual climate, I often have to count the cost of being a Christian constitutional conservative defending liberty. In that vein, I've worked to be a leading voice in the call for a return to faith, the Constitution, and conservative values. This work has proven to be a lonely road—a road that seems to be growing lonelier.

In 2009, after years of playing the game of Republicans "good"/ Democrats "bad" that dominates American politics, I realized that I needed to focus on my Christian

Constitutional Conservative values to, hopefully, put the focus where it belongs: protecting our God-given rights.

The turning point came for me in a unique way.

Several years ago, I attended an event hosted by Wild At Heart Ministries based on a book by John Eldridge. In one session, we were taught about how God will give us a new name to replace the old names given to us by the Devil as a result of our wounded hearts.

At first, the name I heard came as a disappointment to me.

A few days after returning home, however, as my wife and I discussed some political issues of the day over breakfast, she commented that I needed to be talking about these things to all of America. At first, I dismissed the idea. "After all," I told her, "America already has people like Rush Limbaugh, Glenn Beck, and others."

Always an encourager, she mentioned that she saw me as "a voice in the wilderness." With those words, I froze in amazement because, unbeknownst to her, the name I heard at the event was "John the Baptist." Scripture refers to him as "the voice of one crying out in the wilderness." (John 1:23)

So, I took up her challenge and created *The Strident Conservative* blog, where I address the political and religious topics important to conservatives, often with a satirical, irreverent, and politically incorrect perspective. Since then, I have reached millions of people who have read my thoughts and who share my concerns about the state of our nation.

I also secured a position at our local public radio station to learn as much as I could about broadcasting, which led to other opportunities in broadcasting, such as guest hosting for talk radio stations in major markets and the development of a nationally distributed daily two-minute radio feature.

True to the spirit of John the Baptist, I have worked to be a "serrated edge" to the political and spiritual leaders of the world, to be an influence for such a time as this.

To be *strident* means "to be sharply insistent on being heard."[7] John the Baptist was strident with the political and religious leaders of his time, and that's what I strive to do through my work.

Even though the odds are overwhelmingly against me, I chose to continue this fight against the political establishment and the faux-conservative media conglomerates.

I remain committed to fighting for life, freedom of speech, religious liberty, the right of every American to keep and bear arms, our founding principles, limited government, Judeo-Christian values, and fiscal, social, and constitutional conservatism.

And as a non-binary (politically speaking) independent conservative, I will continue drawing comparisons between Republicans and Democrats (though there is little difference between the two anymore) as I endeavor to lead the way for those still lost in the fog.

UNDERSTANDING OUR CONDITION (A&OX3)

When an EMT (Emergency Medical Technician) or paramedic comes upon a trauma victim, one of the first things he or she will do is assess the person's level of consciousness by asking three questions: What is your name? What day is it? Where are you? If these three questions are answered correctly, the trauma victim is considered fully conscious—Alert and Oriented Times Three (A&O×3).

Our country is in trauma, and sadly, too many of her citizens are alert and oriented, times zero. Their understanding of America has been reduced to the fact that she exists, nothing more. They have no comprehension of the severe injuries liberty has suffered or how if nothing is done, these injuries will lead to the death of freedom.

In some instances, a fourth question has been added to the emergency protocol, establishing what is known as Alert and Oriented Times Four (A&O×4): Can you tell me what happened to you? This fourth question gives us another reference point essential to understanding the condition of liberty in America.

We must identify our condition before we can make the necessary changes to return to a heart of liberty. We cannot discover our condition by using the self-interested wisdom provided by a government motivated by its insatiable desire to replace God as the provider of our rights.

We need to resist the temptation to dismiss the seriousness of America's condition. We must become oriented if we are ever to find America's greatness again.

WHO ARE YOU, AMERICA?

Gary Barkalow, founder of The Noble Heart, is an expert on how individuals can live the life they were created to live and how the keys to living that life are forged in the human heart. In "A Dangerous But Necessary Road," a 2009 e-letter, Barkalow shared the following thought:

> I recently overheard a conversation between two men. One said, "The strong rule the weak. That's how your God made the world." The other responded, "God makes us strong only for a while, so that we can help each other." To which the first man responded, "My God makes me strong so I can live my life."

> This conversation was in a movie I re-watched called *First Knight, the King Arthur and Camelot Story.* The first and last man to be quoted was Malagant, the fallen knight from Arthur's Round Table.

> Malagant captured in a sentence the general belief of the era that we are living in— "My God makes me strong so I can live my life." **In a word, this belief can be described as narcissism—and is defined as excessive self-admiration and self-centeredness.** (Emphasis mine)[8]

Though Barkalow is addressing the heart of the individual, his words prompted this question in my mind:

Could it be that America has surrendered liberty to the Republican/Democrat duopoly because she has lost her heart and has become as narcissistic as the politicians in Washington the duopoly repeatedly vote for?

The next part of Barkalow's post answered this question:

Erwin McManus wrote in his book *Stand Against the Wind*, "When we are in love with ourselves, we are prone to listen only to what we want to hear. **We become willing to trade insight for affirmation. We want to feel good about ourselves more than we want to become good**." (Emphasis mine)[9]

The Mayo Clinic describes Narcissistic Personality Disorder, in part, as a mental health condition in which "people have an unreasonably high sense of their own importance. People with this disorder may lack the ability to understand or care about the feelings of others."[10]

Quite simply, America suffers from a similar disorder. She has fallen in love with herself. She has wandered so far from her heart—a heart of God-given liberty—that she no longer desires to hear what she needs to hear but only what she wants to hear. Many Americans have developed an "unreasonably high sense of their own importance," and they "lack the ability to understand or care about the [liberty] of others."[11]

God didn't give America the gift of liberty simply to provide a place for self-centered individuals to live their lives any way they choose. Instead, liberty was given to equip us to live as a nation filled with the desire and passion necessary to realize our calling. It allowed us to be the shining city upon a hill often spoken of by Ronald Reagan, which he highlighted in his farewell address from the Oval Office on January 11, 1989:

> And that's about all I have to say tonight, except for one thing. The past few days, when I've been at that window upstairs, I've thought a bit of the "shining city upon a hill." The phrase comes from John Winthrop, who wrote it to describe the America he imagined. What he imagined was important because he was an early Pilgrim, an early freedom man. He journeyed here on what today we'd call a little wooden boat, and like the other Pilgrims, he was looking for a home that would be free.

> I've spoken of the shining city all my political life, but I don't know if I ever quite communicated what I saw when I said it. But in my mind, it was a tall, proud city built on rocks stronger than oceans, wind-swept, God-blessed, and teeming with people of all kinds living in harmony and peace; a city with free ports that hummed with commerce and creativity. And if there had to be city walls, the walls had doors, and the doors were open to anyone with the will and the heart to get here. That's how I saw it and see it still.[12]

WHAT DAY IS IT?

America has veered from the road that leads to liberty and has plummeted over the cliff of self-centeredness. The guard rails erected by the Founding Fathers to keep us on that road—the US Constitution and the Declaration of Independence—have been destroyed under the misguided and selfish assumption that we are capable enough on our own to maneuver without them.

Going forward, America can get back on that road and find liberty again, but only if Republicans and Democrats in Washington acknowledge the damage they have done to her heart and admit the need for restoration. Liberty won't be found by continuing down the narrow road without the guardrails necessary to avoid crashing off the cliffs.

Our nation needs conservatives willing to work as the road crew to repair the damage and rebuild the guardrails and safeguards because that's the only way we will ever heal America's lost heart of liberty; it won't happen at the hands of those responsible for destroying the road in the first place.

Now *that's* an infrastructure plan I can get behind.

WHERE ARE YOU, AMERICA?

GPS (Global Positioning System) is an amazing bit of technology. A device that easily fits in the palm of your hand can triangulate with multiple satellites 13,000 miles over your head and tell you where you are within a few feet.

To know where we are so that we can navigate our way successfully and accurately through the fog of a world that's diametrically opposed to God-given liberty, we must triangulate using the three documents, known collectively as the Charters of Freedom: The Declaration of Independence, the Constitution, and the Bill of Rights.

> We hold these truths to be self-evident, that all men are created equal, that they are endowed by their Creator with certain unalienable Rights, that among these are Life, Liberty and the pursuit of Happiness. (Preamble of the Declaration of Independence)

> We the People of the United States, in Order to form a more perfect Union, establish Justice, insure domestic Tranquility, provide for the common defence, promote the general Welfare, and secure the Blessings of Liberty to ourselves and our Posterity, do ordain and establish this Constitution for the United States of America. (Preamble of the US Constitution)

> The Conventions of a number of the States, having at the time of their adopting the Constitution, expressed a desire, in order to prevent misconstruction or abuse of its powers, that further declaratory and restrictive clauses should be added: And as extending the ground of public confidence in the Government, will best ensure the beneficent ends of its institution. (Preamble of the Bill of Rights)

The only way out of the fog of confusion, and the only way to find and live in liberty, is to purge America's heart of inaccurate maps and navigational information and triangulate with the three reference points that created our country.

CHAPTER 2

"A REPUBLIC IF YOU CAN KEEP IT"

"What is the most sacred duty and the greatest source of our security in a Republic? An inviolable respect for the Constitution and Laws."[13]

ALEXANDER HAMILTON
(Founding Father)

"But a Constitution of Government, once changed from Freedom, can never be restored. Liberty, once lost, is lost forever."[14]

JOHN ADAMS
(Founding Father, second president of the United States)

"The Constitution of the United States was made not merely for the generation that then existed, but for posterity—unlimited, undefined, endless, perpetual posterity."[15]

HENRY CLAY
(Lawyer, statesman, 9th US secretary of state)

T he source of the quotation used in the title of this chapter comes from a journal kept by James McHenry (1753-1816), a Maryland delegate to the Constitutional Convention of 1787, founding father, and a signer of the US Constitution.

On a page taken from the journal documenting the events of the last day of the convention, McHenry wrote, "A lady asked Dr. Franklin, 'Well Doctor, what have we got, a republic or a monarchy?' 'A republic,' replied the Doctor, 'if you can keep it.'"[16] Then McHenry added, "The Lady here alluded to was Mrs. Powel of Philada."[17]

Many are familiar with the "if you can keep it" quote, but often left out of the story documenting this interaction between Benjamin Franklin and Mrs. Powel is the rest of the conversation between the two. According to delegate McHenry's account of the exchange published in 1803, after Franklin responded to Mrs. Powel's question with "a Republic, if you can keep it," she said, "and why not keep it?" Franklin replied, "Because the people, on tasting the dish, are always disposed to eat more of it than does them good."[18]

The meaning of Franklin's words is twofold. First, he was letting us know that the Constitution was designed to be a blueprint for generations of Americans to follow. Second, he was warning us that the benefactors of this sacred document could very well be the ones who destroy it.

So, this begs the question: Have we kept it or, to paraphrase Benjamin Franklin, have we bitten off more than we can chew?

Over the years, I've concluded that we have failed to adhere to the Constitution; worse, we've devoured everything available to us at the buffet of liberty, leaving us fat and lazy. Instead of making sure there's plenty of liberty for future generations to chew on, we've replaced the gourmet meal provided by the founders with microwaved leftovers in rationed portions.

Allow me to explain this failure by revisiting some of the examples I briefly mentioned in Chapter One.

MISINFORMATION OR FREE SPEECH

In George Orwell's dystopian vision of the future titled *1984*, the Ministry of Truth was created and pretended to be dedicated to the pursuit of truth, when in fact its primary function was to erase the truth of the past and present and replace it with the Party's truth.[19] This was accomplished through the use of doublespeak and Newspeak, languages used to ensure that everyone thought only what the Party wanted them to think and to make it impossible to betray the Party by thinking independent thoughts.

Orwell referred to the all-powerful government as "the Party," and Americans have repeatedly elected–both literally and figuratively–a modern-day version of this entity consisting of Republicans and Democrats, thereby surrendering the power of the people to these tyrants while trusting them to protect and defend the Constitution.

Using Big Brother-styled methods of manipulation, Republicans and Democrats work to convince the populace that they are the only thing standing in the gap between liberty and safety, that they are the guardians of our heritage and the benevolent defenders of our values, worthy of our trust and support.

In such an environment, the people are "programmed" to question themselves before they question the government, and they suppress suspicion by sealing their lips lest they be exposed as spreaders of misinformation or disinformation and, thus, an enemy of the state.

Republicans and Democrats (the Party) have directed their attack on free speech in true bipartisan fashion.

During the Joe Biden presidency, a de facto Ministry of Truth right out of Orwell's *1984*— the Misinformation and Disinformation Governance Board—was established by the Department of Homeland Security to silence people who rejected the White House's talking points concerning COVID-19 and forced vaccinations.[20] Though temporarily "suspended" after receiving backlash for the obvious threat to free speech, the DHS resumed spying on internet users in secret.[21]

Despite claims to the contrary at the time, Biden's war on free speech and social media was evident when he appointed Nina Jankowicz, a Russian disinformation expert easily influenced by partisan ideology when determining the difference between fact and disinformation, as executive director of the new board.

For example, in a June 2020 op-ed for Wired.com, Jankowicz wrote that Facebook groups were destroying America because they were built for privacy.[22] And in an April 2022 interview with NPR, she had this to say about

Twitter after Elon Musk purchased the burgeoning social media company:

> I shudder to think about if free speech absolutists were taking over more platforms, what that would look like for the marginalized communities all around the world, which are already shouldering so much of this abuse, disproportionate amounts of this abuse, and retraumatizing themselves as they try to protect themselves from it, you know, reporting, blocking, et cetera. We need the platforms to do more, and we frankly need law enforcement and our legislatures to do more as well.[23]

Around the same time that Biden was building his Ministry of Truth, Republican Governor Ron DeSantis of Florida signed a bill into law that allowed Floridians to sue social media platforms if they were "unfairly censored" while conveniently leaving out that the law gave the Florida Election Commission authority to levy fines of $250,000 per day on social media companies that deplatformed any candidate running for statewide office and $25,000 per day for candidates running for non-statewide office.

In March 2020, Republican Senator Lindsey Graham introduced the Eliminating Abusive and Rampant Neglect of Interactive Technologies (EARN IT) Act, a bill designed to give the federal government complete authority to grant or deny Section 230 protection for social media platforms based on their "compliance" with arbitrary and ambiguous rules established by the government under the bill.[24]

Saying that he didn't "buy anything" said by tech companies, Graham accused them of only being concerned about not getting sued, and he threatened the industry with legislation that would ultimately strip them of Section 230 protection if his bill failed to pass due to their opposition.[25] And as we all know, nothing says "this is a good bill" like threatening those opposed to it with the hammer and sickle of big government.

A few years later, Graham teamed up with Democrat senator Elizabeth Warren on the Digital Consumer Protection Commission Act, a bill that would create a new agency specifically designed to "regulate" Big Tech companies like Google, Meta, and Amazon.[26] Tech companies would be required to be licensed by this new agency, and the agency would be empowered to revoke said licenses for "non-compliance" issues.

Ironically, Republicans lined up to take down Big Tech and social media because they censored free speech, while Democrats wanted to take them down because they weren't censoring enough speech. Either way, both parties were working together to control the content of social media and destroy the free speech rights of Americans for political benefit.

THE LGBT AGENDA AND RELIGIOUS LIBERTY

Following *Obergefell v. Hodges*, the Supreme Court ruling in June 2015 that legalized same-sex marriage, I wrote an article warning how this unconstitutional decision would ultimately lead to the end of religious liberty in America.[27] Though many accused me of being a homophobic religious zealot, my conclusions were supported by the LGBT community itself. Destroying religious liberty was the end game all along, "The legal struggle for queer rights will one day be a struggle between freedom of religion versus sexual orientation."[28]

A "zero-sum game" is how homosexual activist, law professor, and Equal Employment Opportunity Commission director for Barack Obama, Chai Feldblum, described future legal battles between modern "rights" based on homosexual "orientation" and the traditional American principle of religious liberty. "Gays win, Christians lose," Feldblum said, predicting homosexuals would win most of the legal contests.[29]

Since the *Obergefell v. Hodges* decision, Congress has attempted to enshrine the LGBT agenda into law by amending the Civil Rights Act of 1964 via legislation known as the Equality Act to prohibit so-called discrimination based on gender identity and sexual orientation.[30]

Besides the clear and obvious threat to genuine civil rights and civil liberty, the Equality Act is loaded with a myriad of unintended consequences so egregious that even voices within the pro-LGBT community opposed it for reasons other than religious liberty. "It would eliminate women and girls as a coherent legal category worthy of civil rights protection," said Julia Beck, a self-described radical lesbian feminist and the former law and policy co-chair for Baltimore's LGBTQ Commission.[31]

The Equality Act would require everyone to submit to the LGBT agenda, with churches and religious employers, organizations, and colleges afforded no exceptions. "Religion is no excuse for discrimination when it comes to sexual orientation or gender identity," said Rep. Jerry Nadler (D-NY) when explaining the intention of the legislation.[32]

Although Democrats were the driving force behind these developments, the Equality Act was first introduced in 2019 when Republicans could have stopped it but didn't. In fact, Republicans supported the goals of the Equality Act, which is why they introduced a "conservative alternative" called the Fairness for All Act in December 2019.[33]

The Fairness for All Act would have also amended the Civil Rights Act using the same pro-LGBT language included in the Equality Act but with additional provisions that allegedly protected the convictions of organizations and employers with fifteen employees or less (religious organizations and healthcare providers).[34] Apparently, "conservative" Republicans felt that larger religious organizations weren't entitled to First Amendment protections.

The Equality Act essentially became a moot point in June 2020 when the Supreme Court ruled in a 6-3 decision (*Bostock v. Clayton County*) written by Justice Neil Gorsuch to create a never-existed-before inalienable right to transgenderism in Title VII of the Civil Rights Act that provided no protections for religious liberty.[35]

By the way, Freedom of Religion wasn't the only casualty following *Obergefell v. Hodges*; Freedom of Speech and Freedom of the Press also suffered. For example, a newspaper in Pennsylvania at the time officially banned any and all voices of opposition on the issue of same-sex marriage.[36]

FAKE NEWS OR FREEDOM OF THE PRESS

Joseph Goebbels was a member of the German Nazi Party when he became Adolf Hitler's propaganda minister. His position gave him absolute power over German radio, press, cinema, and theater. Under his guidance, the Nazi government controlled the timing and content of government communications with the German people, censoring any message not approved by the government. Germans could only see what the Nazi hierarchy wanted them to see, hear what they wanted them to hear, and read what they wanted them to read.

Ironically, at the same time that Goebbels was busy destroying the press and the media in Germany, Franklin Delano Roosevelt was doing the same thing in America . . . and for many of the same reasons.[37]

Roosevelt enjoyed a good relationship with the press at the start of his public career, but it quickly unraveled, eventually leading FDR to complain about the press's "poisonous propaganda."[38] This hatred of the media led him to proclaim during his reelection in 1936 that 85 percent of the newspapers were against him. He would later declare that "our newspapers cannot be edited in the interests of the general public, from the counting room. And I wish we could have a national symposium on that question, particularly in relation to the freedom of the press."[39]

In 1938, Sen. Sherman Minton (D), an FDR loyalist who was rewarded for his loyalty with an appointment to the Seventh Circuit Court of Appeals (he was later appointed to the Supreme Court by Harry Truman), led an "investigation" into newspapers that were less than enchanted by FDR's New Deal. Minton would eventually sponsor a bill that made it a crime for newspapers to print any article "known to be false."[40] Of course, it was the government making that determination.

Early in Barack Obama's second term, it was revealed that his administration was using intimidation tactics against the Associated Press and FOX News, which led everyone from the White House to *The New York Times* to demand the passage of new laws to protect the media from government interference when they report on subjects involving the government.[41] Of course, the First Amendment already provides those guarantees, but Washington wasn't about to let a pesky little thing like the Bill of Rights get in the way of an opportunity to "fine tune" the intentions of the Founding Fathers—even if it meant playing the Joseph Goebbels card.

Enter Lindsey Graham, again, and his so-called Media Shield Bill. Graham and co-sponsor Chuck Schumer claimed the bill was directed at protecting national-security information and the rights of journalists to protect the identity of their anonymous sources, but in a meeting with reporters to discuss the bill, Graham expressed his true motivations:

Who is a journalist is a question we need to ask ourselves. Is any blogger out there saying anything—do they deserve First Amendment protection? These are the issues of our times.[42]

Who is a journalist? Can a blogger say anything? I can see how these would be the "issues of our times," but only if you believe it's the government's job to answer those questions.

Under the Media Shield Bill, only government-approved messages would be permitted.[43] Government would have the power to decide who the "real" journalists are and who would be worthy of Constitutional protection. In other words, the media would have essentially become a sanctioned arm of the government instead of the independent guardians of the fourth estate.

In 2018, Donald Trump's Department of Homeland Security (DHS) proposed the creation of a "Media Monitoring Services" division to track hundreds of thousands of news sources, "including: journalists, editors, correspondents, social media influencers, bloggers, etc."[44] In addition to monitoring media content, this new division would have been empowered to make arbitrary judgments on the "sentiment" of those they are tracking.

Speaking of Donald Trump, his presidency became well-known for relying on one of the propaganda tools used by Joseph Goebbels by referring to the news media as "Fake News."[45] Goebbels called the media "Lügenpresse," which translates to "lying press."

Trump also borrowed from Goebbels when he referred to the media as the "enemy of the American people."[46] During the reign of the Third Reich, Goebbels released his "Ten anti-Jewish Commandments," where he called the Jews "a sworn enemy of the German people," who posed a risk to Adolf Hitler's vision for Germany.[47]

Trump's disdain for the media reared its liberty-killing head during the 2016 GOP primaries when he openly promised to eliminate libel laws to remove the media's constitutional protection and make it easier for the government to sue the press and make "lots of money":

One of the things I'm going to do, and this is going to make it tougher for me... but one of the things I'm going to do if I win... is I'm going to open up our libel laws so when they write purposely negative and horrible and false articles, we can sue them and win lots of money. We're going to open up those libel laws. So that when the *New York Times* writes a hit piece, which is a total disgrace, or when the *Washington Post*, which is there for other reasons, writes a hit piece, we can sue them and win money instead of having no chance of winning because they're totally protected.[48]

During the early years of Joe Biden's presidency, Alexandria Ocasio Cortez (AOC) jumped on the "misinformation" train when she proposed creating a government-sanctioned news media to combat so-called misinformation following the January 6, 2021 riots on Capitol Hill.[49]

I think that's an interesting concept for us to explore and I do think that several members of Congress, in some of my discussions, have brought up media literacy, because that is part of what happened here and we're going to have to figure out how we rein in our media environment so that you can't just spew disinformation and misinformation.[50]

THE RIGHT TO BEAR ARMS (SECOND AMENDMENT)

Barack Obama often resorted to using his "pen and phone" to issue executive orders to restrict ownership of certain gun models and ammunition, and he was an early advocate of creating a national gun registry where only those approved by Washington could own a gun.

When Joe Biden first took up residency in the White House, he picked up where Obama left off when he issued a plethora of executive orders of his own to restrict gun ownership and take steps to create a national gun registry.

Biden outlined six measures his administration would pursue to curb gun violence, including instructions for the Department of Justice (DOJ) to create a red-flag-law template for the states to use when writing their own legislation.[51] He also instructed the DOJ to create a national version of the unconstitutional gun-grabbing legislation, complete with making incentives (bribe money) available to states that pass red flag laws of their own.[52]

Biden later issued an order banning some handguns by redefining them as "short barrel rifles" if they were modified with stabilizing pistol braces, a change that subjected handguns to heightened regulations under the 1934 National Firearms Act and laid the foundation for creating a de facto gun registry for these firearms.[53]

Joe Biden claimed that he and the Bureau of Alcohol, Tobacco, Firearms and Explosives (ATF) were operating completely within the confines of the Constitution because, after all, none of our rights are "absolute."

> Nothing I'm about to recommend in any way im-
> pinges on the Second Amendment. They're phony ar-
> guments suggesting these are Second Amendment
> rights at stake with what we're talking about. But no
> amendment, **no amendment to the Constitution is**
> **absolute.**[54] (Emphasis mine)

Donald Trump established himself as an advocate of gun control when he proclaimed in an Oval Office meeting with Republicans and Democrats that police should "take the guns first, go through due process second" as a way to make America safe.[55] During his tenure, Trump openly embraced Nancy Pelosi's gun-control agenda, pushed for enhanced background checks, and proposed expanding red flag laws on a national level—three priorities important to Joe Biden as well.

With pressure from Washington, various states have created "red flag" laws (aka Extreme Risk Protection Orders) to enable law enforcement agencies to seize firearms from individuals who have committed no crime without due process. Having witnessed the "success" of red flag laws at the state level, Senators Lindsey Graham (R) and Richard Blumenthal (D) joined forces to push a bill nationalizing them. Their Federal Extreme Risk Protection Act would give federal courts jurisdiction over the states in matters of gun control.[56]

But the Graham/Blumenthal bill wasn't enough for Marco Rubio. The Republican senator from Florida put red flag laws on steroids when he teamed up with senators Kyrsten Sinema (D) and Thom Tillis (R) to co-sponsor the Threat Assessment, Prevention, and Safety Act of 2019 (TAPS Act).[57] Rubio's TAPS Act would require law enforcement to give *everyone* a personal threat assessment (adults and children) to single out those deemed to be a future threat and then "stop dangerous individuals before they can commit an act of violence."

There was also a House version of the TAPS Act (H.R. 838) co-sponsored by reps. Brian Babin (R-TX) and Val Demings (D-FL).

PROTECTION AGAINST UNREASONABLE SEARCH AND SEIZURE (FOURTH AMENDMENT)

Red flag laws obviously violate the Fourth Amendment, but another way the government violates it is via the out-of-control growth of the surveillance state.

Biometric technology has made it easier for the federal government to improve and expand its mass surveillance capabilities through programs like digital ID cards. Digital IDs gained momentum during the COVID-19 pandemic when they served as the basis for developing digital vaccine passports, but the surveillance state needed more control, which is where digital currency entered the picture.

According to an October 2022 case study provided by World Bank consultant Adam Cooper, a program mixing digital currency and biometrics would create the "digital transformation" necessary to improve mass surveillance of the population.[58] A Central Bank Digital Currency (CBDC) like the one developed by the Federal Reserve and the US government would likely be connected to a social credit system like the one used in communist China.

Experts in the tech industry tell us that the digital platform used to create vaccine passports is the same platform used in China's "social credit system."[59] Some of the areas tracked in real-time by the Chinese Communist Party (CCP) are:

► Medical history
► Social media posts and internet search history
► Bank accounts and credit cards
► Residence, employment, and criminal history
► Relationships and religious activities
► Political activity[60]

CBDCs and social credit scores like those used in communist China would provide the information the government needs to completely control our economic lives, resulting in a complete loss of privacy and liberty, a fact confirmed by the heads of the United States Federal

Reserve and European Central Bank (ECB) in a September 2022 meeting.[61]

Big government and big banks can use CBDCs to routinely and covertly control how people spend their money because digital dollars are traceable, programmable, and can be "printed" at any time. Rules and restrictions are built into their design, literally putting every single cent of our money under government control to be spent (or not spent) as Big Brother sees fit.

DUE PROCESS OF LAW (FIFTH AMENDMENT)

Gun control laws lead the way for the government to violate our right to due process.

In 2013, Barack Obama launched Operation Choke Point.[62] This initiative used banks and financial institutions to track down firearms dealers suspected of illegal activities without the Fourth Amendment's protection against unreasonable search and seizure and the Fifth Amendment's guarantee of due process.

Like just about everything else done under the Obama/Biden administration, Operation Choke Point violated our constitutional rights, which is why it had to be used as a back-door method of dismantling the Second Amendment by using banks to shut down "risky" gun dealers by denying them bank services.

As president, Joe Biden used the "risky" gun dealer argument—he called them "merchants of death" who sell "illegal guns"—to justify banning handguns, building a national gun registry, and pushing to add gun control to the Violence Against Women Act.[63]

In 2015, the Federal Deposit Insurance Corporation (FDIC) released a memo telling banks to essentially ignore Operation Choke Point, but that didn't "officially" happen until 2017 under the Trump administration.[64] However, like many of the actions taken by Donald Trump, canceling Operation Choke Point was more for show because banks were still using it to target firearms dealers as recently as 2018 when Trump and the Republican Party had full control of Washington.[65]

Based on lessons learned from Barack Obama's Operation Choke Point, Joe Biden launched his own plans to use financial institutions to destroy liberty in America. A few weeks after his loss in 2020, Trump and the Republican-controlled Senate proposed expanding the federal government's ability to spy on the bank accounts of every American. Though nothing concrete happened with the Republican proposal at the time, Joe Biden embraced the idea in May 2021 with a plan involving the IRS. In September 2021, he provided details for a scheme I referred to as a Patriot Act for the IRS—giving that government agency the ability to track every aspect of our financial lives.[66]

Biden's plan provided $80 billion and 87,000 new agents to the IRS for spying on the finances of any person for any reason at any time. These surveilled people were neither suspected of a crime nor were they permitted to opt out of this data collection. Still, Biden's plan required the government to preemptively tag and track their financial transactions as if they had done something wrong.

STATES' RIGHTS (TENTH AMENDMENT)

Gun control. Abortion. Gay "rights." Mass surveillance. These are just a few of the areas in recent history where the federal government has routinely violated states' rights and the rights of the people in the name of advancing its agenda.

- ► **Gun control:** See above

- ► **Abortion:** For decades, *Roe v. Wade* was considered the "law" of the land even though, as the Supreme Court ruled in *Dobbs v. Jackson* (2022), abortion wasn't protected in the US Constitution.[67] Roe denied the God-given right to life referenced in the Declaration of Independence, and it prevented the states from passing laws to protect the unborn.

- ► **Gay "rights":** As I mentioned earlier, the Supreme Court ruling in *Obergefell v. Hodges* has gradually led to the destruction of religious liberty, but it first destroyed the right of the states to define and regulate marriage under the Tenth Amendment.

- ► **Mass surveillance:** See above.

In hindsight, it is evident that our constitutional republic has substantially eroded from what the Founding Fathers intended when they signed their names to the Constitution on that historic day in 1787. If we are ever to rediscover the founding principles of that sacred document, we must first better understand what the founders had in mind when they enshrined them. Then we can hopefully reconnect to how it all began.

WHERE WE BEGAN

"If you do not know where you come from, then you don't know where you are, and if you don't know where you are, then you don't know where you're going. And if you don't know where you're going, you're probably going wrong."[68]

SIR TERRY PRATCHETT

Author, humorist, satirist

CHAPTER 3

THE BASICS

"Those of us who shout the loudest about Americanism, are all too frequently those who . . . ignore some of the basic principles of Americanism - the right to criticize, the right to hold unpopular beliefs, the right to protest, the right of independent thought."[69]

MARGARET CHASE SMITH

(First woman to serve in both houses of Congress)

"What makes it possible for politicians to do so many things that are economically counterproductive is that neither the public nor the media know enough of the basics to understand what's wrong with what they're saying."[70]

THOMAS SOWELL

(Economist, social philosopher, political commentator)

"Any fool can know. The point is to understand."[71]

ALBERT EINSTEIN

(German physicist)

A t the start of training camp in July 1961, the late, great coach of the National Football League's Green Bay Packers, Vince Lombardi, took a fascinating approach to training his players in preparation for the new season.

The legendary coach wasted no time getting straight to the point, and in a manner that struck fear and dread in the hearts of each of his players, he delivered one of the greatest one-liners of all time.

With a football firmly in his hands, Lombardi walked to the front of the room, taking several seconds to look at his men in total silence. Just when the silence had become almost unbearable, the American football legend held up the pigskin and said, "Gentlemen, this is a football."[72] With those five simple words, Lombardi communicated his point: We're going to start with the basics.

Those men, most of whom had played football in college before becoming professionals, knew what a football was, and they most likely had a good understanding of the game itself. But the man who would set records as one of the most successful coaches in NFL history—a man so revered that the Super Bowl trophy is named after him—believed that any knowledge they had of the game was insufficient without a firm understanding of the basics.

We, the people of the United States, are much like that room full of players. We may think we understand what liberty looks like, but over the 200-plus years we have been a nation, we have lost sight of the basics established by the Founding Fathers.

If they were alive today, I can almost imagine Thomas Jefferson or James Madison standing before us, wanting to ensure that we experience the success we were destined to achieve, holding the document up for all to see and saying, "America, this is the Constitution."

Understanding the basics helps us to know what we had and what we have lost. So what are the basics?

> We hold these truths to be self-evident, that all men are created equal, that they are endowed by their Creator with certain unalienable Rights, that among these are Life, Liberty and the pursuit of Happiness. That to secure these rights, Governments are instituted among Men, deriving their just powers from the consent of the governed. (Preamble of the Declaration of Independence)

> We the People of the United States, in Order to form a more perfect Union, establish Justice, insure domestic Tranquility, provide for the common defence, promote the general Welfare, and secure the Blessings of Liberty to ourselves and our Posterity, do ordain and establish this Constitution for the United States of America. (Preamble of the United States Constitution)

In the words of Thomas Jefferson, liberty is an endowment given to us by our Creator. Jefferson calls God-given liberty a "truth" (which means that it is considered a fact) that is "self-evident" (which means it requires no proof or explanation). In other words, liberty comes from God, period!

But knowing where the source of liberty comes from doesn't tell us what it looks like, which is why James Madison, with input from Jefferson, authored the first ten amendments to the Constitution, known collectively as the Bill of Rights.

> The Conventions of a number of the States, having at the time of their adopting the Constitution, expressed a desire, in order to prevent misconstruction or abuse of its powers, that further declaratory and restrictive clauses should be added: And as extending the ground of public confidence in the Government, will best ensure the beneficent ends of its institution. (Preamble of the Bill of Rights)

With these basics firmly understood, the Founding Fathers gave us what we needed to protect liberty in America.

If focusing on fundamentals helped Vince Lombardi create a football dynasty, can you imagine how focusing on the basics of liberty could do the same for American greatness? Instead of focusing on electing politicians based on party labels or promises of "goodies," we should be crying out for men and women dedicated to the fundamentals of liberty.

The Constitution's power relies solely on "we the people" and our belief in its power. After all, the Constitution itself is just a piece of paper; it only has the power to protect liberty if we collectively know and understand the basics and then apply that understanding. If we don't, how can we expect our government to do so? Our failure only ensures our demise.

Washington politicians, regardless of party affiliation, love to take the Constitution out of context to expand their power. Our job is to know and understand the basics so we can call out those in power who abuse the Constitution for political benefit and either hold them accountable or replace them. We can also, hopefully, enlighten those around us who have bought into the propaganda their politicians are feeding them.

CHAPTER 4

THE PLACE FOR LIBERTY

"Is life so dear or peace so sweet as to be purchased at the price of chains and slavery? Forbid it, Almighty God! I know not what course others may take, but as for me, give me liberty, or give me death!"[73]

PATRICK HENRY
(Founding Father)

"Where the people fear the government, you have tyranny. Where the government fears the people, you have liberty."[74]

JOHN BASIL BARNHILL
(Indictment of Socialism, Barnhill-Tichenor Debate on Socialism)

"You will never know how much it has cost my generation to preserve your freedom. I hope you will make a good use of it."[75]

JOHN ADAMS
(Founding Father, second president of the United States)

"Liberty is the breath of life to nations."[76]

GEORGE BERNARD SHAW
(Playwright, political activist)

To better understand the importance of liberty, we need to take a closer look at how and why the Founding Fathers made it central to the formation of America and why we need to keep it central to our existence today.

Many important colonists opposed the idea of severing ties with Britain even though they saw King George III as a tyrant who treated them unfairly. But that changed in January 1776 when Thomas Paine's forty-seven-page pamphlet titled *Common Sense* was published.

Paine's work condemned the injustices suffered under a king's rule, and he used it to argue that Americans needed to take advantage of the opportunity they had to change their destiny by creating a new government where they could live in liberty and rule themselves.[77] Some of the points made by Paine were:

► **Government should exist for the people, not the people for the government.** The British system failed to do that because it gave the monarchy all of the power.

► **Having a king was a terrible idea.** Paine's opinion of a monarchy was so low that he wrote: "Of more worth is one honest man to society and in the sight of God, than all the crowned ruffians that ever lived."[78]

► **America was a land of freedom.** "This new world hath been the asylum for the persecuted lovers of civil and religious liberty from every part of Europe."[79]

- ► America had been given a once-in-a-lifetime opportunity to create a new nation based on liberty and self-rule.

- ► A call for creating a strong central government governed by a constitution that protected individual rights, including freedom of religion.

By the spring of 1776, *Common Sense* had convinced many colonists that independence from Britain was a good idea after all, and it would serve as the inspiration for Thomas Jefferson to write the Declaration of Independence.

The level of commitment demonstrated by the fifty-six men who attached their signatures to the Declaration shows that, as Abraham Lincoln declared in the Gettysburg Address over eighty years later, a nation "conceived in liberty" exceeds anything we see in our government today.

The Founding Fathers risked it all to create the United States of America. It was a remarkable gamble because most of them were wealthy, successful men. They didn't fight a war against England for personal or financial gain; they fought it because they sincerely believed that the loss of liberty was worse than death.

And for the support of this Declaration, with a firm reliance on the protection of Divine Providence, we mutually pledge to each other our Lives, our Fortunes, and our sacred Honor. (Excerpt from the Declaration of Independence)

LIBERTY OR FEAR

Fear is a real and legitimate emotion, but when the government uses it to its own advantage to protect and grow its power, society falls into what the famous essayist Montesquieu described as despotism, where the government wields absolute power over its citizens. This is exactly what the Founding Fathers were dealing with in the case of King George III. Fear paralyzes. Fear neutralizes. Fear is perhaps the most powerful weapon used by tyrannical governments to silence and control the masses.

In his book, *The Spirit of the Laws*, Montesquieu detailed how a spirit of fear must be present for despotism to survive and thrive.[80] If a despot or dictator fears the people, his tyrannical powers are limited, but if he succeeds in getting the people to fear his power, he can force them to do as he wishes.

Conversely, liberty motivates. Liberty inspires the passion and commitment we need to live in freedom as defined in the Declaration of Independence and protected by the Constitution. Liberty and fear aren't necessarily mutually exclusive, but they can't coexist equally. We either surrender to fear and allow tyranny to rule, or we embrace liberty and the Constitution regardless of the consequences.

Throughout history, liberty in America has been under assault by despots and tyrants, but the assaults intensified after the terrorist attacks on September 11, 2001. At that time, George W. Bush and a nearly unanimous Congress used the fear of terrorism to bring us the PATRIOT Act and other liberty-killing laws.

This assault on liberty gained new power during the so-called COVID-19 pandemic of 2020-2022, where the government used fear of the virus to launch an unprecedented assault on liberty. Mixing the fear-mongering of COVID-19 with the growing acceptance of socialist and Marxist ideology, liberty-killing policies were passed or proposed by both Republicans and Democrats, not letting the COVID-19 "crisis" go to waste, thus allowing them to do things they were unable to do before.

Over time, Nationalist Republicans—they incorrectly refer to themselves as conservatives—have come to believe many of the same things as their Democratic Socialist counterparts. They both preach that the "evils" of capitalism and individualism are responsible for the ills of society and that a bigger and more powerful government is needed to protect our right to live our lives as we choose.

This is the America we live in after years of assault on liberty and the Constitution by the Republican/Democrat duopoly, an assault that intensified during the presidencies of both Donald Trump and Joe Biden.

Republicans want conservatives to believe that nationalism and populism (a watered-down word often used to describe fascism) can make America great again, provided we get rid of Democrats and their Marxist/socialist ideals. But the bottom line is this: unless we dedicate ourselves to the Constitution and reject party politics, our republic will not survive.

CHAPTER 5

THE CHRISTIAN ROOTS OF LIBERTY

"The highest glory of the American Revolution was this: it connected in one indissoluble bond the principles of civil government with the principles of Christianity."[81]

JOHN QUINCY ADAMS

(Sixth president of the United States)

"I have lived, Sir, a long time and the longer I live, the more convincing proofs I see of this truth—that God governs in the affairs of men. And if a sparrow cannot fall to the ground without his notice, is it probable that an empire can rise without his aid? We have been assured, Sir, in the sacred writings that 'except the Lord build they labor in vain that build it.' I firmly believe this; and I also believe that without his concurring aid, we shall succeed in this political building no better than the Builders of Babel."[82]

BENJAMIN FRANKLIN

(Founding Father, diplomat, political philosopher)

"We have no government armed with power capable of contending with human passions unbridled by morality and religion ... Our Constitution was made only for a moral and religious people. It is wholly inadequate to the government of any other."[83]

JOHN ADAMS

(Founding Father, second president of the United States)

"The God who gave us life gave us liberty. Can the liberties of a nation be secure when we have removed a conviction that these liberties are the gift of God?"[84]

THOMAS JEFFERSON

(Founding Father, author of the Declaration of Independence, third president of the United States)

The relationship between Christianity and the US Constitution has been a topic of debate from the beginning of America's existence. It has been argued by some that the Constitution was written by secular-minded deists who sought to create a society neutral on matters of God and religion, while others have held to the belief that the Constitution was based on Christian values.

Sure, some of the founders were deists, but the vast majority went on the record to declare that religious faith was essential to the formation of the self-sustaining republic they were creating.

Consider the words of Noah Webster, an American Founder and the Father of American Education, when he said: "[T]he Christian religion, in its purity, is the basis, or rather the source of all genuine freedom in government . . . and I am persuaded that no civil government of a republican form can exist and be durable in which the principles of that religion have not a controlling influence."[85]

Clearly, a reliance on God and the Christian faith was foundational to the creation of the United States of America and its survival as a land of liberty. Unfortunately, the church of today has ignored this fact, choosing instead to trade liberty and the Gospel of Jesus Christ for political power and influence.

I wrote an article in 2016 documenting how America's religious leaders were little different than the Nazi German religious leaders ultimately responsible for the rise of Adolf Hitler using, in part, an excerpt taken from *Bonhoeffer*, a biography recounting the life of Dietrich Bonhoeffer in Germany (1906-1945), written by Eric Metaxas.[86] In Timothy J. Keller's foreword for the book, we read:

> It's impossible to understand . . . without becoming acquainted with the shocking capitulation of the German church to Hitler in the 1930s. How could the 'church of Luther' . . . ever come to such a place? The answer is that the true gospel, summed up by Bonhoeffer as 'costly grace,' had been lost. On the one hand, the church had become marked by formalism. That meant going to church and hearing that God just loves and forgives everyone,

so it doesn't really matter much how you live. Bonhoeffer called this 'cheap grace.' On the other hand, there was legalism, or salvation by law and good works. Legalism meant that God loves you because you have pulled yourself together and are trying to live a good, disciplined life. **Both of these impulses made it possible for Hitler to come to power.**[87] (Emphasis mine)

The church in 1930s Germany was a house divided, with one side preaching an "anything goes" abuse of God's grace, and the other side preaching that salvation was based on the law and good works. It was the acceptance of these false gospels that created the vacuum filled by Adolf Hitler. Church "leaders" on both sides admitted that there were things about Hitler that bothered them, but not enough to risk losing their comfortable existence and the special "favors" he doled out for their allegiance.

It has long been my assertion that the spiritual condition of the twenty-first-century church so closely resembles that of 1930s Germany that we are dangerously close to seeing liberty fall at the hands of a Hitler-like leader.

In 2016, the "cheap grace" evangelical leaders I have come to refer to as the Fellowship of the Pharisees supported Donald Trump in much the same way that the 1930s German church supported Hitler. As a reward for their servitude to "God's Man," they were given seats at his table where they would fight for the crumbs of power he offered. The Fellowship often mentioned things about Trump's immoral behavior and policies that bothered them, but not enough to risk losing their seats at his table.

Much like the Laodicean church spoken of in the Book of Revelation, today's cheap-grace evangelicals have become lukewarm and lazy as they bask in their so-called riches, not realizing that they are pitiful blind beggars who will be vomited out of Jesus' mouth.

In a 2020 study released as part of the Cultural Research Center (CRC) of Arizona Christian University's American Worldview Inventory, we see just how far today's evangelicals have fallen.[88] In the words of George Barna:

> The most startling realization regarding the theological reformation in progress is how many people from evangelical churches are **adopting unbiblical beliefs**. What makes that trend so significant is that evangelical churches, by definition, teach that the Bible is the authoritative word of God that teaches not only salvation by grace alone but also an array of life principles that are meant to drive one's thoughts and actions.[89] (Emphasis added)

Here are some of the unbiblical beliefs reflected in the 2020 report on these four faith families: evangelicals, Pentecostals and charismatics, mainline Protestants, and Catholics (Emphasis added):

► Evangelicals are embracing secularism: A majority (52%) of evangelicals **reject absolute moral truth**; 61% do not read the Bible on a daily basis; 75% believe that people are basically good. The study found that one-third to one-half of evangelicals in the survey **embrace a variety of beliefs and behaviors counter to biblical teaching and long-standing Evangelical beliefs.**

► Pentecostals and Charismatics take secularization a step further: Two-thirds (69%) **reject absolute moral truth**; 54% are **unwilling to define human life as sacred**, with half claiming the **Bible is ambiguous in its teaching about abortion**; 69% saying **they prefer socialism to capitalism**; and a full 45% did not qualify as born-again Christians.

► Mainline Protestants are the most secular of the four faith families: A majority (60%) of mainline Protestants' **beliefs directly conflict with biblical teaching**. Three key values define this group: **truth and morality are relative; life has no inherent value or purpose**, so individuals should pursue personal happiness or satisfaction; and traditional religious practices are no longer seen as central or essential to their Christian faith. Only 41% of mainline Protestants are born again.

► Catholics are increasingly secular and permissive: Catholics' beliefs are surprisingly similar to those of mainline Protestants but considerably different from that of evangelical and charismatic Protestants. They are most likely to believe in **salvation through works or living a good life**, and least likely (28%) to be born again. Today's Catholics are more permissive than other groups, being most **likely to accept sexual relations outside of marriage, lying, speeding, and refusal to repay a loan as morally acceptable behaviors.**[90]

Concerning Catholics, by the way, I also wrote in 2020 about how Pope Francis had begun promoting Marxist ideology as a key tenet of Catholicism—advancing socialism and attacking private property rights while calling for the institution of global wealth redistribution.[91]

In Bonhoeffer's day, Germany fell victim to the rise of the National Socialist German Workers Party (Nazi Party), and the people lost their right to life and liberty as a result. The cheap-grace gospel of the 1930s lukewarm church created the environment that made that possible.

In today's America, we are also losing our rights to life and liberty at the hands of governmental policies and practices that embrace a form of socialism. And just as it was in the 1930s, the church is largely responsible. Catholics and Protestants of every stripe have replaced the Gospel of Jesus Christ with a cheap-grace counterfeit—spreading socialism and immorality while systematically destroying faith . . . and, as a result, liberty in America.

CHAPTER 6

THE ORIGINS OF CONSERVATISM

"The basis of conservatism is a desire for less government interference or less centralized authority or more individual freedom...."[92]

— RONALD REAGAN

(40th president of the United States)

"Conservatism, we are told, is out-of-date. This charge is preposterous and we ought to boldly say so. The laws of God, and of nature, have no dateline. These principles are derived from the nature of man, and from the truths that God has revealed about His creation. To suggest that the Conservative philosophy is out of date is akin to saying that the Golden Rule, or the Ten Commandments or Aristotle's Politics are out of date."[93]

— BARRY GOLDWATER

(US Senator, 1964 Republican Party nominee for president)

"There is nothing wrong with describing conservatism as protecting the Constitution, protecting all things that limit government. Government is the enemy of liberty. Government should be very restrained."[94]

RON PAUL

(Texas congressman, libertarian activist)

"Conservatism starts from a sentiment that all mature people can readily share: the sentiment that good things are easily destroyed, but not easily created."[95]

— SIR ROGER VERNON SCRUTON

(Editor of The Salisbury Review, a conservative political journal)

The origins of conservatism go back to the late 18th century following the radical upheaval of the French Revolution, but the modern American conservative movement began in the 1930s in response to Franklin Delano Roosevelt's New Deal and the increasingly oppressive Democrat machine.

After decades of Democratic control of national politics following World War II, the conservative movement took hold of Washington in 1980 with the election of Ronald Reagan.

President Ronald Reagan breathed life back into the conservative movement with massive tax cuts, a new emphasis on building a strong national defense, deregulation of business, confronting communism, and advancing policies based on family values and Judeo-Christian morality. But in the days and years since Reagan's second term came to an end, conservatism in America, particularly within the Republican Party, has lost its bearings.

The root word of conservative is *conserve*. Conservatives are supposed to work to conserve the principles of our God-given rights to life, liberty, and the pursuit of happiness and the Constitution designed to protect those rights. Since these rights come from God and not the government, conservatives have the added responsibility to conserve morality. As John Adams once said, "Our constitution was made only for a moral and religious people. It is wholly inadequate to the government of any other."[96]

Conservatism is neither a cause nor a measurable standard; it's a way of life. It is a set of morally, fiscally, socially, and politically sound values that form our deeply held convictions. It's an unshakable commitment to the principles handed down to us in the Declaration of Independence and the US Constitution by the Founding Fathers—principles that have made America the greatest nation on Earth.

ESSENTIAL PRINCIPLES OF CONSERVATISM

► **Individual Liberty**—The concept that all Americans are endowed by their Creator with the inalienable right to life, liberty, and the pursuit of happiness.

► **Individual Responsibility**—The idea that human beings choose, instigate, or otherwise control their own actions. As a result of our actions, we are held morally accountable or legally liable.

► **Limited Government**—The US Constitution was created to limit the power and scope of government to ensure liberty and maintain a civil society.

► **States' Rights**—Federal government control is the antithesis of individual liberty. The Founding Fathers knew that solutions to the challenges we would face would have to be attained voluntarily and locally.

- ► **Fiscal Responsibility**—Government must live within its means and pursue appropriate levels of spending to maintain sustainable public finances without borrowing or raising taxes.

- ► **Defense of the Constitution and Bill of Rights**—Designed by the Founding Fathers, these documents guarantee our God-given liberty and provide an intricate system of government checks and balances that ensure those freedoms.

- ► **Defense of Life**—Every single human life, from conception until natural death, is designed by God for a purpose and is entitled to the same inherent freedoms as every American—above all, the freedom to live.

This is but a brief introduction to the origins of the American conservative movement, but to paraphrase the words of the ancient Athenian historian and general, Thucydides, "Knowledge for its own sake [is] meaningless, its mere accumulation a waste of time. Knowledge must lead to understanding."[97]

In other words, it's not enough to have knowledge about the history of conservatism; we must allow knowledge to lead us to a better understanding of where conservatism is today. Without this knowledge, we'll be unable to chart a new course into the future.

WHERE WE ARE NOW

"To understand reality is not the same as to know about outward events. It is to perceive the essential nature of things. The best-informed man is not necessarily the wisest. Indeed there is a danger that precisely in the multiplicity of his knowledge he will lose sight of what is essential. But on the other hand, knowledge of an apparently trivial detail quite often makes it possible to see into the depths of things. And so the wise man will seek to acquire the best possible knowledge about events, but always without becoming dependent upon this knowledge. To recognize the significant in the factual is wisdom."[98]

DIETRICH BONHOEFFER

(Theologian, anti-Nazi revolutionary,
founder of the Confessing Church)

CHAPTER 7

THE EVOLUTION OF CONSERVATISM

"It's not a conservatism rooted in a government philosophy. It is more cultural in the sense of outrage politics, left-versus-right, us-versus-them. It is not about whether government is going to be involved. It is more along the lines of: 'Government is going to be involved. Who is going to get the spoils of government?'"[99]

— KEVIN MADDEN

(Advisor for Mitt Romney's 2012 presidential campaign)

"I'm conservative, but I'm not a nut about it."[100]

GEORGE H. W. BUSH

(41st president of the United States)

"I call my philosophy and approach compassionate conservatism."[101]

GEORGE W. BUSH

(43rd president of the United States)

"I fought against long odds in a deep blue state, but I was a severely conservative Republican governor."[102]

MITT ROMNEY

(Republican Party's 2012 nominee for President)

Conservatism has evolved into something it was never intended to be. I suspect that is perhaps one of the greatest understatements of all time.

In a lame attempt to curry the favor of conservatives without actually being conservative, many within the Republican Party use modifiers designed to give the impression that they are something they obviously are not. Christian conservative. Social conservative. Fiscal conservative. Libertarian conservative. Labels like these are meant to imply that conservatism can be modified while still protecting our values. These modified labels are little more than lipstick on a pig—a cosmetic change meant to disguise the true nature of their faux conservatism.

The Republican party has also "updated" conservatism using a mixed bag of "isms" that have further destroyed liberty:

► **Nationalism**: Though often confused with patriotism, it's neither patriotic nor conservative. It's racist and socialistic.

Nationalism is synonymous with powerful big government. The driving purpose of nationalists is to secure more power and control. An example of what this looks like can be seen in a keynote speech given by Sen. Josh Hawley (R-MO) at the 2019 National Conservatism Conference, where he called for a "new conservatism" and attacked the "powerful upper class and their cosmopolitan priorities."[103]

▶ **Socialism**: The polar opposite of conservatism. Merriam-Webster dictionary defines socialism as a political and economic theory of social organization that advocates that the means of production, distribution, and exchange should be owned or regulated by the community as a whole and controlled by the government.[104] Unfortunately, nationalists have embraced much of the socialist agenda, creating what I've come to call "conservative socialism."

▶ **Populism**: Often referred to as "tyranny by majority," this political ideology allows the common people to be exploited by the privileged elitists they voted for. Though traces of populism can be seen in just about any political party, it became a dominant feature in the Republican Party following the 2016 election of Donald Trump. When paired with nationalism, populism creates a system diametrically opposed to the limited-government principles that have been at the heart of conservatism.

▶ **Economic Nationalism**: A protectionist ideology where the government assumes complete control of the economy and allows tariffs and other restrictions on trade, labor, goods, and capital—both foreign and domestic. Economic nationalism is antithetical to conservatism's free market and limited government principles.

▶ **Fascism**: A form of government characterized by an authoritarian central power resulting in an infringement on liberty. It's essentially the culmination of nationalism, as we witnessed in a speech given by Gov. Ron DeSantis at the 2022 National Conservatism Conference.

During his hour-long speech, DeSantis condemned the Republican Party's handling of big business and told attendees that the party needed to follow his example, saying that his experience as Florida governor proved to be a "lesson for people on the right."[105]

"Corporatism is not the same as free enterprise, and I think too many Republicans have viewed limited government to basically mean whatever is best for corporate America is how we want to do the economy," DeSantis said before accusing "corporate America" of having too much power and "exercising quasi-public power in terms of using their economic power to change policy in this country."[106]

"What I'm doing is using government to give space to the individual citizen to be able to participate in society to be able to speak his or her mind," DeSantis said.[107] "And I think that's an absolutely appropriate use of government power."

Contrary to the Republican Party's redefinition of conservatism, their hyphenated labels and "isms" will never succeed at protecting liberty in America. They will, however, provide the party with the political cover necessary to advance their liberty-killing agenda.

CHAPTER 8

9/11, THE PATRIOT ACT, AND THE NEW AXIS OF EVIL

"These [NSA] programs were never about terrorism: they're about economic spying, social control, and diplomatic manipulation. They're about power."[108]

— EDWARD SNOWDEN

(Whistleblower who exposed National Security Agency spying)

"The Patriot Act is the most egregious piece of legislation to ever leave Congress since the Alien and Sedition Acts. John Ashcroft and every member of Congress who voted for it should be indicted."[109]

— MICHAEL BADNARIK

(2004 Libertarian Party nominee for President of the United States)

"Voice or no voice, the people can always be brought to the bidding of the leaders. That is easy. All you have to do is tell them they are being attacked and denounce the pacifists for lack of patriotism and exposing the country to danger. It works the same in any country."[110]

HERMANN GOERING,

Germany Reborn (Nazi war criminal)

"If Tyranny and Oppression come to this land, it will be in the guise of fighting a foreign enemy."[111]

JAMES MADISON

(Founding Father, fourth president of the United States)

S peaking before the American people in his 2002 State of the Union address, President George W. Bush presented his strategy for how America would respond to the new threat to liberty facing us in the aftermath of the terrorist attacks on the World Trade Center and the Pentagon on September 11, 2001. In his speech, Bush identified three countries as being primarily responsible for this threat: North Korea, Iraq, and Iran. He labeled these enemies "an axis of evil."[112]

> Our second goal is to prevent regimes that sponsor terror from threatening America or our friends and allies with weapons of mass destruction.
>
> Some of these regimes have been pretty quiet since September 11, but we know their true nature. North Korea is a regime arming with missiles and weapons of mass destruction while starving its citizens.
>
> Iran aggressively pursues these weapons and exports terror, while an unelected few repress the Iranian people's hope for freedom.
>
> Iraq continues to flaunt its hostility toward America and to support terror. The Iraqi regime has plotted to develop anthrax and nerve gas and nuclear weapons for over a decade.
>
> States like these, and their terrorist allies, **constitute an axis of evil** . . .[113] (Emphasis added)

In the face of this very real threat, America responded to Bush's call to prevent regimes that sponsor terror from threatening America, our friends, and allies with weapons of mass destruction. Sadly, as the passing of time has led us to forget the events of that terrible day, the resolve to defeat the axis of evil has waned, and the threat to freedom has returned with a vengeance from these same nations.

As history draws ever closer to repeating itself, the words of Winston Churchill in the days leading up to World War II ring true:

> When the situation was manageable, it was neglected, and now that it is thoroughly out of hand we apply too late the remedies which then might have effected a cure. There is nothing new in the story. It is as old as the Sibylline books. It falls into that long, dismal catalogue of the fruitlessness of experience and the confirmed unteachability of mankind. Want of foresight, unwillingness to act when action would be simple and effective, lack of clear thinking, confusion of counsel until the emergency comes, until self-preservation strikes its jarring gong-these are the features which constitute the endless repetition of history.[114]

International terrorism is a very real threat to our God-given liberty and freedom, but there is another that is just as insidious and even more devious. It has been at work for decades yet has gone mostly undetected because it has been working from within the system.

Like a wolf in sheep's clothing, this new threat has been stealthily at work undermining the very foundations of liberty endowed to us by "(our) Creator," as penned in the Declaration of Independence by Thomas Jefferson and, in piecemeal fashion, it has been steadily working to destroy the Constitution and our "unalienable rights."

Using the governmental structure established in the beginning by our Founding Fathers—Executive, Legislative, and Judicial branches—this new threat has brought America to the precipice of the total destruction of liberty.

From the American Revolution to wars in the Middle East, from communism to radical Islam, these three branches of American government, meant to protect and preserve liberty and freedom, have instead become tools to bring oppression and the loss of freedom.

I call these three branches . . . The New Axis of Evil.

SEPTEMBER 11, 2001—THE DAY LIBERTY DIED IN AMERICA

When we annually recognize the terrorist attacks that took place in New York City and Washington, D.C., on September 11, 2001, we are reminded of many things. We remember the thousands of innocent lives that were lost and the billions of dollars in economic damage. But as great and tragic as these losses were, another loss continues to be the greatest of all—the loss of liberty.

The demise of liberty didn't occur at the hands of the hijackers; it occurred at the hands of the New Axis of Evil. The Transportation Security Administration (TSA). The PATRIOT Act. The PATRIOT Act II. National Security Agency (NSA) spying. Fake cell phone towers being used to tap your cell phone. These are just a few examples of how the government of, by, and for the people has become the government over, above, and beyond the people.

As the list of post-9/11 changes above shows, George W. Bush, the president who "abandoned free market principles to save the free market system," could have just as easily stated that he was willing to abandon freedom to save freedom post-9/11.[115] While it was popular at the time to blame Barack—Terrorism? What terrorism?—Obama for the situation, we must remember that this particular attack on liberty began under Bush. There are many who say Bush's intentions were purer than the presidents who succeeded him, but they are mistaken.

Just days before the anniversary of 9/11 in 2014, the US DOJ released two memos detailing the Bush administration's legal justification for monitoring the phone calls and emails of Americans *without a warrant* under a secret program dubbed Stellar Wind that began after the

September 11, 2001 attacks. "Even in peacetime, absent congressional action, the president has inherent constitutional authority ... to order warrantless foreign intelligence surveillance," then-assistant attorney general Jack Goldsmith said in a heavily redacted 108-page memo dated May 6, 2004.[116]

> We believe that Stellar Wind comes squarely within the commander-in-chief's authority to conduct the campaign against Al-Qaeda as part of the current armed conflict and that congressional efforts to prohibit the president's efforts to intercept enemy communications through Stellar Wind would be an unconstitutional encroachment on the commander in chief's power.[117]

Checking ... checking ... checking ... Nope! It's not in the Constitution. In fact, the Fourth Amendment to the Constitution says the exact opposite:

> The right of the people to be secure in their persons, houses, papers, and effects, against unreasonable searches and seizures, shall not be violated ... no Warrants shall issue, but upon probable cause, supported by Oath or affirmation, and particularly describing the place to be searched, and the persons or things to be seized.

Sounds pretty clear to me.

Post-Bush, the Axis of Evil grew more powerful when the next Republican president moved into the White House in 2016. Under the leadership of Donald Trump and the Republican Party, the US Cyber Command—an idea originally proposed by Barack Obama—was created within the NSA to give the agency greater power to spy on Americans. Trump also reauthorized FISA-702, which allowed the NSA to conduct warrantless electronic surveillance on Americans.

The government's liberty-killing agenda took off post-9/11, but their tyrannical reaction to COVID-19 took it to places previously unimagined under the PATRIOT Act.

In a piece I wrote in March 2020 about how COVID-19 was leading America to the end of liberty and the beginning of tyranny, I referenced an article written by John Whitehead, the founder and president of the Rutherford Institute.[118] It is Whitehead's contention (and mine as well) that COVID-19 tyranny was leading America down the road to becoming a full-blown police state.

This coronavirus epidemic, which has brought China's Orwellian surveillance out of the shadows and caused Italy to declare a nationwide lockdown, threatens to bring the American Police State out into the open on a scale we've not seen before.

If and when a nationwide lockdown finally hits—if and when we are forced to shelter in place—if and when militarized police are patrolling the streets—if and when security checkpoints have been established—if and when the media's ability to broadcast the news has been curtailed by government censors—if and when public systems of communication (phone lines, internet, text messaging, etc.) have been restricted—if and when those FEMA camps the government has been surreptitiously building finally get used as quarantine detention centers for American citizens—if and when military 'snatch and grab' teams are deployed on local, state, and federal levels as part of the activated Continuity of Government plans to isolate anyone suspected of being infected with COVID-19—and if and when martial law is enacted with little real outcry or resistance from the public—then we will truly understand the extent to which the government has fully succeeded in recalibrating our general distaste for anything that smacks too overtly of tyranny.

This is how it begins.[119]

Socialist policies and the tyranny they create became the norm during the so-called pandemic.

Donald Trump's daughter and advisor on economic matters, Ivanka, had her feminist, socialist dream of government-mandated paid family leave become a reality when one of the first coronavirus bailouts—Families First Coronavirus Response Act—included taxpayer-funded paid family leave and provisions for taxpayer-funded sick leave.[120] Other socialist-based policies such as prison reform, gun control, and Alexandria Ocasio-Cortez's Green New Deal also experienced major advances.

The events of 9/11 brought us the PATRIOT Act, so it was with a bit of irony that COVID-19 tyranny brought us a Patriot Act for healthcare, a plan created by Trump's son-in-law and advisor, Jared Kushner. Kushner envisioned forming a government/private-sector partnership to create a new "surveillance and data collection system" to track coronavirus Americans.[121] Parts of Kushner's vision became reality when vaccine passports were jointly developed by a group of health and technology companies under the belief that governments and businesses would eventually require proof of being vaccinated before being allowed to return to "normal."

The Axis of Evil's use of COVID-19 to destroy liberty continued under Joe Biden. On the 20th anniversary of 9/11, Biden identified a new terrorist threat: Americans exercising their God-given, constitutionally protected right to free speech to criticize the government's COVID-19 policies. In a terrorism threat advisory released in 2021 by Biden and his Department of Homeland Security (DHS), it was determined that people pushing "anti-government rhetoric," including people standing in "opposition to COVID-19 measures," would be classified as "domestic terrorists."[122]

The advisory lumped people exercising their free speech rights via online forums, people who disagreed with COVID-19 restrictions, and Al-Qaeda into one all-encompassing category. In the eyes of Joe Biden, exercising your free speech right to protest masks and vaccine mandates and/or using social media to do so made you no different than the terrorists who crashed planes into the Pentagon and the World Trade Center on 9/11.

From Bush to Biden after 9/11, Washington made killing liberty in the name of safety standard operating procedure.

CHAPTER 9

SLAVES IN THE WASHINGTON MATRIX

"The ideal tyranny is that which is ignorantly self-administered by its victims. The most perfect slaves are, therefore, those which blissfully and unawaredly enslave themselves."[123]

DONALD JAMES

(British writer and novelist)

"The accumulation of all powers, legislative, executive, and judiciary, in the same hands, whether of one, a few, or many, and whether hereditary, self-appointed, or elective, may justly be pronounced the very definition of tyranny."[124]

JAMES MADISON

(Founding Father, fourth president of the United States)

"The Matrix is everywhere. It is all around us. It is the world that has been pulled over your eyes to blind you from the truth. A prison for your mind."[125]

LAURENCE FISHBURNE

as Morpheus in The Matrix

"Man is born free; and everywhere he is in chains."[126]

JEAN-JACQUES ROUSSEAU

(Philosopher, writer)

Why does liberty feel more like a fairy tale than reality? Because we are looking at it through the eyes of the Axis of Evil instead of through the eyes of the Constitution and the Declaration of Independence. Deep down inside, we know something is wrong, but we've been citizens of the system for so long that we no longer realize we've become slaves. We get a picture of what this looks like in an early scene taken from the science-fiction movie *The Matrix*, where Morpheus and Neo meet for the first time:

Morpheus: I can see it in your eyes. You have the look of a man who accepts what he sees because he's expecting to wake up. Ironically, this is not far from the truth. Do you believe in fate, Neo?

Neo: No.

Morpheus: Why?

Neo: Because I don't like the idea that I'm not in control of my life.

Morpheus: I know exactly what you mean. Let me tell you why you're here. You're here because you know something. *What* you know you can't explain. You feel it. You've felt it your entire life. There's something wrong with the world. You don't know what it is. But it's there, like a splinter in your mind, driving you mad. It is this feeling that has brought you to me. Do you know what I'm talking about?

Neo: The Matrix?

Morpheus: Do you want to know what it is?

[Neo nods his assent]

Morpheus: The Matrix is everywhere. It is all around us. Even now in this very room. You can see it when you look out your window, or when you turn on your television. You can feel it when you go to work, when you go to church, when you pay your taxes. It is the world that has been pulled over your eyes to blind you from the truth.

Neo: What truth?

Morpheus: That you are a slave, Neo. Like everyone else, you were born into bondage, into a prison that you cannot taste or smell or touch. A prison for your mind. Unfortunately, no one can be told what the Matrix is. You must see it for yourself.[127]

If you've seen the movie, you know that Morpheus offers Neo the choice of taking the blue pill of the status quo or the red pill of truth. Neo takes the red pill, and he frees himself from the slavery of the Matrix.

The Matrix is a parable, but it tells a story that's eerily reminiscent of the reality we are living in America, which is why the tale resonates so strongly with me. Like Neo, we have become subjects in a Matrix-like system that enslaves us for its own benefit while depriving us of our birthrights of life and liberty. Like Neo, things aren't what they seem. But also, like Neo, we can be set free of the bondage of the system if we choose to be.

Morpheus didn't hand Neo his deliverance on a silver platter. Instead, he offered him an invitation. Neo could choose to remain in the safety of the system or take the risk of breaking free of it to join the war against the Matrix.

Likewise, liberty won't be handed to us on a silver platter, but we can accept the invitation to leave the safety of a system owned and operated by the Republican/ Democrat duopoly and take the risk of breaking free of it by joining the war for liberty against the new Axis of Evil.

CHAPTER 10

TRADING MORALITY FOR POLITICAL POWER

"If immorality prevails in the land, the fault is ours in a great degree. If there is a decay of conscience, the pulpit is responsible for it. If the public press lacks moral discrimination, the pulpit is responsible for it. If the church is degenerate and worldly, the pulpit is responsible for it. If the world loses its interest in religion, the pulpit is responsible for it. If Satan rules in our halls of legislation, the pulpit is responsible for it. If our politics become so corrupt that the very foundations of our government are ready to fall away, the pulpit is responsible for it... Let us not ignore this fact, my dear brethren; but let us lay it to heart, and be thoroughly awake to our responsibility in respect to the morals of this nation."[128]

CHARLES G. FINNEY

(Minister, leader of the Second Great Awakening in the US)

"Religion today is not transforming people; rather it is being transformed by the people. It is not raising the moral level of society; it is descending to society's own level, and congratulating itself that it has scored a victory because society is smilingly accepting its surrender."[129]

A. W. TOZER

(Pastor, author, magazine editor, mentor)

"We do not want ... a church that will move with the world. We want a church that will move the world."[130]

G.K. CHESTERTON

(Writer, author, Christian apologist)

BLACK RELIGIOUS LEADERS CALL TO NATIONALIZE POLICE

I n the wake of the August 2014 tragic fatal shooting of Michael Brown in Ferguson, Missouri, a group of religious and civil rights leaders joined the Congressional Black Caucus and signed an open letter calling on Barack Obama and the Justice Department to take "immediate action" to implement policy changes to local law enforcement, including demands to essentially nationalize local police departments.[131] The letter said, in part:

> Michael Brown, an unarmed African American teen shot multiple times and killed by a Ferguson, Mo police officer, is only the latest in a long list of black men and boys who have died ... Investigations into the Ferguson shooting are ongoing, and many of the specific facts remain unclear for now. However, the pattern is too obvious to be a coincidence and too frequent to be a mistake.[132]

The letter then demanded several actions be taken by Obama and the DOJ, including:

► Racial bias training for every police department in the country using guidelines set by the DOJ as a part of ongoing professional development and training.

► Removing the ability of local police departments to conduct internal investigations and establish national standards created and implemented by the DOJ for conducting such investigations.

► Creating new diversity standards using best practices established by the DOJ to implement and monitor diversity hiring and retention guidelines for local police departments.

► The appointment of a federal (national) czar, housed in the DOJ and specifically tasked with promoting the professionalization of local law enforcement, monitoring egregious law enforcement activities, and adjudicating suspicious actions of local law enforcement agencies that receive federal funding.[133]

Though these demands sat on the back burner for a short time, they received new attention in April 2015 when riots took place in Baltimore, Maryland, following the death of Freddie Gray while in police custody, thus giving Barack Obama another opportunity to push for the nationalization of local law enforcement via a special connection he had with the mayor. Mayor Stephanie Rawlings-Blake was a key player in Barack Obama's plan to federalize the nation's police force when she served as one of three mayors on his Task Force on 21st Century Policing, which advocated for federal control of law enforcement in exchange for government funds.[134]

It was at this time that Rev. Al Sharpton, an advisor to Barack Obama, renewed his call for having the federal government take over local police, as reported by Newsbusters.org:

> "We need the Justice Department to step in and take over policing in this country. In the 20th century, they had to fight states' rights in—to get the right to vote. We're going to have to fight states' rights in terms of closing down police cases."[135]

EVANGELICALS EXCHANGE G-O-D FOR G-O-P

During the presidency of Bill Clinton, Evangelicals made character one of the primary qualifications for being president, and they openly criticized Clinton for his failures in this department. He was, according to Evangelical leaders at the time, a lying, draft-dodging womanizer unfit to serve as the leader of our great nation.

But all of that changed when another lying, draft-dodging womanizer, this time with an "R" after his name, ran for the office. Surrendering their convictions for convenience and a seat at Herod's table, Evangelicals abandoned morality in favor of moral relativism to support Donald Trump.

In the summer of 2016, Donald Trump held a closed-door, media-free meeting with a group of Evangelicals and prosperity gospel con-artists to discuss the terms of their surrender to his holiness—I call Trump his holiness because he has lived such a perfect and sinless life that he never felt it necessary to ask God for forgiveness.[136]

Mike Huckabee, the multi-failed GOP candidate for president and a reverend (kind of like how Al Sharpton and Jesse Jackson are reverends), was one of the moderators of the get-together, and he made it quite clear that Trump's morality—or immorality—would be taken off the table. "I don't think anybody came here today expecting you to be able to answer a Bible quiz. That wasn't the point," Huckabee said before adding, "You're off the hook on deep theological questions."[137] Huckabee then praised the twice divorced, thrice-married, unrepentant, pro-Planned Parenthood, adulterous strip-club owner for his "family values."

Ralph Reed, the founder and chairman of the Faith and Freedom Coalition and co-conspirator in the Jack Abramoff tax-evasion scandal, was in attendance and expressed his support for Trump by declaring that Christians who refused to vote for Trump as a matter of their convictions were "guilty of the sin of pride."[138]

A few weeks before the 2016 election, a 1995 recording of Trump bragging about how he could "grab [women] by the p*ssy" and get away with it because he was "a star" made national headlines.[139] Up until that moment, Evangelicals had used a wide range of excuses for defending Trump's indefensible and immoral behavior—from "we aren't voting for a pastor-in-chief" to "Jesus isn't on the ballot"—all in the name of electing "not Hillary." While this revelation should have been the proverbial "line in the sand" that no Christian should cross, it actually fired them up to the point of openly defending sexual assault.

Michele Bachmann, the former congresswoman from Minnesota who was serving as Trump's religion advisor when she declared that he was "raised up by God" to be president, blamed the media for this revelation of his sexual abuse.[140] And Trump's running mate, Mike Pence, sounded a lot like a leftist defending abortion when he said that he was personally "offended" by Trump's comments and that he didn't defend or condone them, but he didn't condemn them either.[141]

It wasn't much of a surprise to hear "Christians" within the campaign defend Trump's sexual assaults, but it was quite disturbing to hear some of the national voices of the Evangelical community do so. Tony Perkins, leader of the Family Research Council, defended his unconditional support of Trump by saying that his decision to do so wasn't based on "shared values."[142] And Ralph Reed dismissed the video as insignificant compared to "real issues" like the economy.[143]

Other moral relativists in the Evangelical movement who abandoned morality at the time to defend Trump included several members of the Fellowship of the Pharisees, such as Franklin Graham, Eric Metaxas, Robert Jeffress, and James Dobson.

2020: THE CHURCH OF LAODICEA ENDORSES TRUMP'S REELECTION

After spending all of Trump's first term defending his indefensible behavior and preaching their lukewarm cheap-grace theology, Evangelical leadership turned things up a notch during Trump's 2020 reelection campaign by adding the prosperity gospel to its repertoire. The love of money may be the root of all evil, but it comes in pretty handy when you're trying to win an election for God's chosen immoral candidate.

The Fellowship of the Pharisees and their friends in the faux-conservative media promoted the idea that Trump had created what he called "the greatest economy in history" and was, therefore, worthy of another term in office despite his complete lack of moral character.[144] Who cares, after all, that Trump is an immoral man who habitually lies and breaks his promises?

We're getting paid!

But let's put the economy aside for a moment. When Evangelicals compromised their values for mammon under the mistaken belief that money covers a multitude of sins, they officially turned Washington into the city of Laodicea and the Church of Jesus Christ into the Laodicean church. The Book of Revelation, 3:15-17, explains:

> I know you inside and out, and find little to my liking. You're not cold, you're not hot—far better to be either cold or hot! You're stale. You're stagnant. You make me want to vomit. You brag, 'I'm rich, I've got it made, I need nothing from anyone,' oblivious that in fact you're a pitiful, blind beggar, threadbare and homeless. (The Message)

Lukewarm Evangelicals are dangerously and eternally wrong to think money and a healthy economy are all we need to consider when voting.

CHRISTIANS HAVE A "MORAL OBLIGATION" TO SUPPORT TRUMP

As the 2020 election drew closer, Evangelicals began equating support for Trump to worshiping God. In other words, if you want to be a moral person doing God's perfect will, you must support Donald Trump; doing otherwise was essentially a sin.

In a book written by Ralph Reed, Christians were told that they "[had] a **moral obligation** to enthusiastically back" Trump in 2020.[145] (Emphasis added) According to his publisher, Regnery Publishing, an imprint of Salem Media Group, Reed's book was originally titled *Render to God and Trump*, an obvious reference to the words of Jesus when he said, "Render to Caesar the things that are Caesar's and to God the things that are God's."[146] However, equating Trump to Caesar was apparently too close to the truth for the pro-Trump publisher, so they changed the title to *For God and Country: The Christian Case for Trump* without providing an explanation.[147]

Regnery also said Reed's book would rebut claims that Evangelical Protestants had "revealed themselves to be political prostitutes and hypocrites" for supporting Trump as well as claims that those who had "so thoroughly compromised their witness that they are disqualified from speaking out on moral issues."[148]

TRUMP'S ABUSE OF POWER SCANDAL

In 2019, Donald Trump was impeached (the first of two times) for "abuse of power" after engaging in extortion in a failed attempt to force Ukraine to help his reelection and "obstruction of Congress" for refusing to comply with Congress' subpoenas and requests for documents and testimony.[149] With their seats at Herod-Trump's table firmly secured, and with Trump's 2020 reelection looking less likely, the Fellowship went right to work building a "hedge of protection" around their orange messiah by defending and praising him for his god-like character.

In an appearance on Tony Perkins' *Washington Watch* program, Michele Bachmann, who was chairwoman of Perkins' Family Research Council before working for Trump, defended Trump against impeachment, saying that he "understands the difference between good and evil."[150] Additionally, she said, "We have not seen a president with greater moral clarity than this president."[151]

Based on some of her previous statements, Bachmann's defense was somewhat subdued. Earlier in 2019, she said in an appearance on *Understanding the Times* that Trump was "highly biblical" and that we'll "never see a more godly, biblical president again in our lifetime."[152]

First Baptist Church of Dallas pastor Robert Jeffress, who predicted a "civil war" if Trump were impeached and once called "Never Trump" Evangelicals "spineless morons" for not supporting him, appeared on Fox Business with Lou Dobbs to defend Trump for "the values [he] embraces."[153,154]

Jeffress also trumpeted that "99 percent of evangelicals oppose[d] impeachment" because "never in the history of America have we had a president who was a stronger warrior for the Judeo-Christian principles upon which this nation was founded than in President Donald J. Trump."[155] The Southern Baptist Pharisee also said that "the effort to impeach President Trump is really an effort to impeach our own deeply held faith values."[156]

From the very beginning and continuing throughout his presidency, Trump's unethical and immoral behavior was on full display, yet the Fellowship of the Pharisees and so-called Evangelicals continued to defend him, destroying faith and trading morality for political power.

THE GREAT SHAKING

In the 1980s, numerous scandals were brought to light involving several well-known American evangelists, including Jim Bakker, Jimmy Swaggart, Peter Popoff, and Robert Tilton. These Evangelical leaders defended their immoral behavior by using God's Word, particularly passages dealing with grace and forgiveness.

During the rise of Nazi Germany, Dietrich Bonhoeffer recognized that the church in his day had become ineffective due to their refusal to call evil by name and their over-reliance on what he referred to as "cheap grace," which he defined as forgiveness without repentance.[157] As I mentioned earlier in this book, the parallels between the Evangelical churches of today and the church of Nazi Germany are frighteningly similar.

Evangelical leaders defended Trump's immorality, thus calling evil good, and God will expose them for destroying the testimony of the church. Much like the 1980s, the majority of them have been or will be removed from their self-centered, politically motivated positions of power. Remember, there will be those to whom Jesus will say, "I never knew you." (Matthew 7: 21-23)

CHAPTER 11

REPLACING GOD WITH GOVERNMENT

"Once abolish the God, and the government becomes the God. That fact is written all across human history; but it is written most plainly across that recent history of Russia; which was created by Lenin. There the Government is the God, and all the more the God, because it proclaims aloud in accents of thunder, like every other God worth worshipping, the one essential commandment: 'Thou shalt have no other gods but Me.'"[158]

G.K. CHESTERTON
(Writer, author, Christian apologist)

"Government is not reason; it is not eloquence. It is force. And force, like fire, is a dangerous servant and a fearful master."[159]

GEORGE WASHINGTON
(Founding Father, first president of the United States)

"We live in a society in which all transcendent values have been removed and thus there is no moral standard by which anyone can say right is right and wrong is wrong."[160]

CHARLES W. COLSON
(Political advisor to Richard Nixon, founder of Prison Fellowship)

THE NEW AXIS OF EVIL

THE GOSPEL ACCORDING TO JERRY BROWN

"**W**.W.J.D. What Would Jesus Do?" This simple message, often found on wristbands and T-shirts, has served as a reminder to Christians to rely on Jesus to guide and direct their paths. It turns out, however, that the "J" in WWJD doesn't stand for Jesus. It stands for Jerry (Brown).

That's right; the part-time Catholic-Zen-Buddhist and full-time left-wing extremist knows exactly what Christians should do . . . at least when it comes to illegal immigration.[161, 162]

In a 2017 interview with Chuck Todd on *Meet the Press*, Jesus—I mean Jerry—told the host that building a wall and deporting illegals was unChristian. "I thought we had to treat the least of these as we treat the Lord. So, I hope [Trump] would reconnect with some of his conservative evangelicals, and they'll tell him that these are human beings and they're children of God, they should be treated that way," said Brown.[163]

I completely see his point. After all, as the governor of the state that routinely leads the nation in murdering the unborn, Jerry most certainly knows how a Christian should treat "the least of these," not to mention California's LGBT indoctrination of children, the decriminalization of child prostitution, and the sexual abuse of children through "transing" them.

OPPOSING THE PARIS CLIMATE AGREEMENT "DISHONORS GOD"

When Donald Trump threatened to withdraw America from the Paris Climate Accord in the early days of his presidency, Nancy Pelosi let the world know that doing so wasn't only wrong, it was an ecological and environmental sin against God and his creation.[164]

"The Bible tells us that to minister to the needs of God's creation is an act of worship," Pelosi said at the time.[165] "To ignore those needs is to dishonor the God who made us, and that is just what we are doing by walking away from this accord."

In apparent obedience to scripture's command that everything "be established by the testimony of two or three witnesses" (2 Corinthians 13:1), Brown supported Pelosi in a "60 Minutes" interview when he blamed the California wildfires on those who deny "the truth" about global warming.[166] He went on to say that Trump and the GOP don't "fear the Lord" or "the wrath of God" when it comes to environmental policies.

Ironically, Pelosi's status as a part-time Catholic might have had something to do with her theological claim. In 2015, Pope Francis issued a papal encyclical urging Catholics everywhere to take action to end global warming. Stressing the effects of global warming on the poor, Pope Francis said, "I don't know if (human activity) is the only cause, but mostly, in great part, it is man who has slapped nature in the face. We have, in a sense, taken over nature."[167]

Climate change is the religion of environmental extremists, and the name of the god they worship is government.

OBAMACARE IS GOD'S WILL AND DEFUNDING PLANNED PARENTHOOD ALSO "DISHONORS GOD"

During a round of debates on healthcare reform in 2017, Nancy Pelosi equated healthcare and abortion to climate change when she informed the world that Obamacare was God's will and that any healthcare bill defunding Planned Parenthood would "dishonor the God who made us."[168]

> So, this is God's creation, we have a real responsibility to it... to minister to the needs of God's creation is an act of worship. To ignore those needs is to dishonor the God who made us ...[169]

Pelosi's sermonettes succeeded in winning over a few converts. Trump and the Republican Party not only failed to repeal Obamacare, but they also provided Planned Parenthood with record levels of taxpayer funds each of the four years Trump was in office.[170] Additionally, Trump's promise to withdraw from the Paris Climate Accord turned out to be fake news because Republicans went to work on ways to advance the global warming agenda.

Many assumed Pelosi was speaking of the God of Abraham, Isaac, and Jacob—the God who sent His only begotten Son, Jesus, to earth as a man to, as C.S. Lewis once wrote, "enable men to become sons of God"—but that's not how this works.[171] Pelosi was talking about the god known as "government."

THE "ALMIGHTY" USE OF EXECUTIVE ORDERS

In Christendom, God is often referred to as the "Almighty God" in recognition of his absolute power over all things. Similarly, the god known as government parades as if it has absolute power over all things concerning liberty. Just as the Christian God is called the Father, the government god is called the President. One of the ways that the Christian God decrees his will is via the written word. Likewise, the government god decrees its will via the written word using what is commonly referred to as the executive order.

Executive orders have been used by presidents ever since George Washington (he issued a total of eight in eight years) to manage government operations, but in today's America, they have become a liberty-killing tool used by tyrannical presidents, both Republican and Democrat, to do as they wish without regard to the checks and balances required by the Constitution.

Barack Obama announced in early 2014 that he wouldn't wait for Congress to create the legislation he needed to advance his agenda, choosing instead to usurp the House and the Senate via decrees written by his "pen and phone":

> We're not just going to be waiting for legislation in order to make sure that we're providing Americans the kind of help they need. I've got a pen and I've got a phone.[172]

Calling Obama's "pen and phone" threat "executive order tyranny," Judge Andrew Napolitano explained the president's motivation:

> In a menacing statement at a cabinet meeting last month . . . the president has referred to his pen and his phone as a way of suggesting that he will use his power to issue executive orders, promulgate regulations and use his influence with his appointees in the government's administrative agencies to continue the march to transform fundamentally the relationship of the federal government and individuals to his egalitarian vision when he is unable to accomplish that with legislation from Congress.[173]

Also chiming in at the time about Obama's executive overreach was none other than Donald Trump, who accused him of "subverting the Constitution for his own benefit," and Mike Pence, who said that Obama's use of executive orders to do as he wished "[was] not leadership."[174, 175]

However, Trump would take "subverting the Constitution" to new heights once in office.

In his first three years as president, Trump's pen and phone created more executive orders than we witnessed under Obama—a trend that continued as he entered the home stretch of his 2020 reelection campaign due to COVID-19.[176]

Trump latched onto executive power as a means to advance his non-conservative agenda while routinely going where no predecessor had gone before. But in so doing, he's also laid a foundation for Joe Biden to build on in areas like gun control and the LGBT agenda.

There can be little doubt that the government has replaced God as the source of liberty with devastating consequences to the social structure of America. This reality is evident in America's willingness to trade liberty for security and safety. Now government operates under the assumption that it can do anything, anytime, for any reason to advance its liberty-killing, tyrannical agenda.

Government is God, and God is government—the two are interchangeable.

And as time has passed, the government god has expanded control over our lives, bringing us ever closer to the complete destruction of liberty.

WHERE WE ARE GOING

"When you see that in order to produce, you need to obtain permission from men who produce nothing; When you see that money is flowing to those who deal, not in goods, but in favors; When you see that men get richer by graft and by pull than by work, and your laws don't protect you against them, but protect them against you; When you see corruption being rewarded and honesty becoming a self-sacrifice; You may know that your society is doomed."[177]

AYN RAND,
Atlas Shrugged

CHAPTER 12

USING CRISES TO GROW THE AXIS OF EVIL

"Of all tyrannies, a tyranny sincerely exercised for the good of its victims may be the most oppressive. It would be better to live under robber barons than under omnipotent moral busybodies. The robber baron's cruelty may sometimes sleep, his cupidity may at some point be satiated; but those who torment us for our own good will torment us without end for they do so with the approval of their own conscience."[178]

C. S. LEWIS
(British writer, theologian)

"History has seen many who claim to be [the] deliverer and saviour of the people. They might come with force and violence and parade their might and splendour as conquerors. The pharaohs of Egypt, Sennacherib king of Assyria, Nebuchadnezzar of Babylon, Darius of Persia, Alexander the Great, Hannibal, Napoleon, Clive of India, Bismarck, the Kaiser, Hitler, Stalin. The story and scene is always the same. They claim to deliver the people from bondage and to establish justice, freedom and peace. They come in might, riding in splendour, dragging prisoners."[179]

REVEREND JOHN C.B. MYER
(A Collection of His Sermons, #1)

"Crisis is the rallying cry of the tyrant."[180]

JAMES MADISON
(Founding Father, fourth president of the United States)

T here can be no doubt that the new Axis of Evil has grown since 9/11, nor can there be any doubt that liberty has been one of the casualties. It's also an indisputable fact that the government has used a variety of crises, both real and manufactured, to accomplish its tyrannical ambitions while systematically dismantling many of our God-given, constitutionally protected rights. To better understand how this happened and how it will ultimately lead to the end of liberty, we need look no further than the COVID-19 "pandemic" of 2020-2022.

When COVID-19 first began making headlines, I suggested that it would be the *pièce de résistance* of Democratic Socialists and Republican Nationalists—an excuse to spend trillions of dollars to finance a big-government agenda after it had been used to create new entitlements, explode the national debt, give convicts a get-out-of-jail-free card, and advance the socialist dreams of both parties.[181] As we now know, there was a brief period of playing the political blame game where Republicans and Democrats tried to out-socialism each other before choosing to join forces and create the largest redistribute-the-wealth stimulus bill in history with the $2.2 trillion Coronavirus Aid, Relief, and Economic Security (CARES) Act.[182]

Though decorated with a $1,200 bow in the form of a check paid directly to taxpayers to make it prettier, the CARES Act was a poorly wrapped, ugly package of bailouts, tax breaks, and kickbacks for big-money donors and special interests that did little to help the victims of the economic crisis created by our "representatives."

But fixing the problem wasn't really their objective; the goal of the CARES Act and subsequent stimulus/bailout legislation was to spread big-government socialism.

Immediately after passing the CARES Act, discussions began on another $2-trillion stimulus package to finance so-called infrastructure improvements.[183] Trump had previously negotiated with Democrat leaders Chuck Schumer and Nancy Pelosi to "get something done on infrastructure in a big way," and COVID-19 hysteria created the perfect environment to help them reach their goal.[184] Though not passed while Trump was in office, Joe Biden's COVID-19-inspired infrastructure bill became law in the first year of his presidency at a cost of $1 trillion, complete with a laundry list of Axis of Evil priorities.

COVID-19 gave America tyranny on steroids, where the government of, for, and by the people was replaced by a government that no longer derives its powers from the consent of the people.

A PATRIOT ACT FOR HEALTHCARE

In the early days of COVID-19, Donald Trump put his son-in-law and senior advisor, Jared Kushner, in charge of his coronavirus task force. In one of his first orders of business, Kushner went to work to create what became known as a Patriot Act for Healthcare.[185]

In the $2.2 trillion CARES Act, over $150 billion was earmarked for financing for hospitals, medical equipment, and healthcare worker protection. Hidden in that number was $1.5 billion for the Centers for Disease Control (CDC) to help state and local governments buy equipment **and other measures** to mitigate the virus' spread. Included in the list of "other measures" was $500+ million to launch a new "surveillance and data collection system" to gather information on how the virus is spreading.[186]

Ivanka's husband teamed up with a number of health technology companies to form partnerships and create a national coronavirus surveillance system capable of giving the government real-time information about where patients seek treatment and for what, creating a huge expansion of the government's use of individual patient data and lowering the bar on our right to privacy during a real or imagined national "crisis."

Apple and Google were two of the early tech companies to join forces with the government, and together they built a so-called "opt-in" contact tracking tool using Bluetooth technology intended to help public officials, aka the government, spy on Americans 24/7. The tool used your smartphone to log everyone you came in close contact with and exchanged contact information with them automatically and anonymously—even people not using the app. If one of those contacts reported having COVID-19 symptoms to the authorities, you were given notification to take action.

VACCINATION RECORDS CARDS AND DIGITAL VACCINE PASSPORTS

As various COVID-19 mandates and lockdowns swept the nation, one of the programs created during the Trump presidency was the vaccination record card issued by the CDC to track your compliance with vaccine mandates.[187] The CDC claimed at the time that the cards were only intended to help Americans keep track of their vaccination schedule, but the reality was that they laid the foundation for digital COVID-19 vaccine passports that would essentially give government control of our daily lives.[188]

The foundation was laid during the Trump administration, but it was Joe Biden who got the ball rolling on the federal COVID-19 vaccine passport program. One of his first executive orders instructed federal agencies to evaluate the idea of creating digital certificates for all vaccinated US citizens.[189] Regardless of the inevitable loss of liberty and the expansion of government tyranny, Biden's COVID-19 passports were designed to be the "new normal" and mandatory, giving the government the ability to track our every move.

Following Biden's executive order, he appeared before the American people and threatened to enforce vaccine mandates by launching a Gestapo-styled police state that would "go community-by-community, neighborhood-by-neighborhood, and ofttimes door-to-door, literally knocking on doors" to get people vaccinated.[190]

White House Press Secretary at the time, Jen Psaki, defended Biden's threat when she told CNN's *New Day*, "What we're trying to do here at the federal government is protect the American people and save lives."[191] One day later, Health and Human Services Secretary Xavier Becerra declared that "it is absolutely the government's business" to know people's vaccination status, arguing the federal government had a vested interest in keeping Americans safe.[192]

For those ready to criticize me again for using the terms "gestapo" and "police state," let me share something with you from the Holocaust Encyclopedia:

> The Gestapo was the political police force of the Nazi state.
>
> Political policing is a specific type of police work. Its goal is to **maintain the political status quo**. Political police forces **protect a state or government** from subversion, sabotage, or coup. **They use surveillance and intelligence gathering**. These methods help them **identify domestic threats against the government**. Political police forces are sometimes referred to as "secret police." **Authoritarian states**, such as the Nazi regime, **often rely on them to maintain and protect their power**.[193] (Emphasis mine)

CDC SPIES ON AMERICANS BY TRACKING CELL PHONES

In the Spring of 2022, we learned how the vaccine passport technology developed under Jared Kushner's guidance using his PATRIOT Act-inspired solution to COVID-19 was used by the CDC under Joe Biden as a back door to spy on Americans without their knowledge or permission.

The CDC obtained cell phone location data as a means of monitoring schools and churches to identify who was or wasn't complying with lockdowns and other mandates, along with more general purposes.[194] The CDC bought access to location data harvested from tens of millions of phones in the United States to perform analysis of compliance with curfews, track patterns of people visiting K-12 schools, and specifically monitor the effectiveness of policy in the Navajo Nation, according to CDC documents obtained by Motherboard Tech by Vice.[195]

This revelation of CDC spying followed earlier news of similar spying by the Department of Homeland Security, the post-9/11 creation of George W. Bush and the Republican/Democrat Axis of Evil, where DHS used real-time cell phone geolocation data to track people, a practice they said was perfectly legal and required no warrant. And a year prior to the DHS program, the Defense Intelligence Agency—there's a contradiction in terms—manipulated parts of the PATRIOT Act to create a program to spy on us via our cell phones without a warrant.

These revelations about the CDC spying on millions of Americans through their cell phones didn't happen in a vacuum; the agency laid the foundation for it with its push for vaccine passports.

SCHOOLS USE REMOTE LEARNING TO SPY ON CHILDREN

School districts across the country faced deadly consequences when they decided to shut down schools and force children to learn at home during COVID-19, creating an explosion in student suicides. The obvious response to this news should have been to fully reopen schools across the nation, but sadly, the tyrannical government decided that spying on your kids via their government-issued remote learning computers was a better way to tackle the issue.[196]

Turning a child's home into a makeshift internment camp for remote learning was literally killing our children. As Dr. Katarina Lindley, a Texas physician who lived in Yugoslavia as a child, wrote in an opinion piece for the *Center Square* in August 2020, remote learning was also deadly to liberty:

> These events remind me of my challenging childhood
> in Yugoslavia—which was characterized by govern-
> ment control and the suppression of individual free-
> doms. Sadly, the U.S. is inching in that direction with
> every additional pandemic rule and restriction. I
> wake up every morning wondering how many rights
> we will lose today in the name of fighting COVID.[197]

The remote learning model and the subsequent increase in child suicides created a so-called unintended opportunity for schools to control more of your children's lives by spying on them through their government-issued remote learning computer.

For example, a new artificial intelligence (AI) software program used by the Clark County School District in Nevada made spying on your kids as easy as clicking a mouse.[198] Using a new technology called GoGuardian Beacon, this AI program monitored every student's school-provided laptop and tablet in search of certain words or other information it believes will lead to self-harm. If it found any, it alerted a teacher who then notified the police to visit the home of the student to do a "wellness check."[199]

EVANGELICALS EMBRACE COVID TYRANNY AND THE DESTRUCTION OF LIBERTY

Religious liberty was one of the casualties in the Axis of Evil's war against life, liberty, and the pursuit of happiness during COVID-19, and as is the case in every war, there were POWs. I call these POWs "Coronavirus Christians."[200]

These prisoners were conditioned to accept the lie that unconstitutional government mandates and the destruction of religious liberty were simply the price they needed to pay for "survival." Instead of defending religious liberty, Coronavirus Christians preached government tyranny as a new kind of theology, where refusing to wear a mask and/or not being vaccinated for COVID-19 proved that you were neither a Christian nor pro-life.[201]

Some of these POWs twisted this new theology to such an extent that they defended COVID-19 vaccines, masks, and government mandates on eschatological grounds, accusing those concerned about the abuse of government power of being peddlers of end-times conspiracy theories.

In a live-streamed keynote address to the 2020 Lawyers' Convention sponsored by the Federalist Society, Supreme Court Justice Samuel Alito noted how government overreach in response to COVID-19 had "resulted in previously unimaginable restrictions on individual liberty."[202] And on the subject of religious liberty, Alito pointed out how the government had "blatantly discriminated against houses of worship" and had put religious liberty "in danger of becoming a second-class right."[203]

"It pains me to say this, but in certain quarters, religious liberty is fast becoming a disfavored right," said Alito before adding this warning about the future, "Whatever one may think about the COVID-19 restrictions, we surely don't want them to become a recurring feature after the pandemic has passed."[204]

In hindsight, Alito's words were prophetic, as the government—often with a little help from coronavirus Christians—took their war against religious liberty directly to houses of worship to engage in a little hand-to-hand combat.

One of those battles occurred during Holy Week within the boundary of our neighbor to the north when Calgary pastor Artur Pawlowski, who had already been fined for feeding the homeless in violation of social distancing rules, took a stand for religious liberty and the gospel when he ordered Canadian police officers to leave his church when they tried to disrupt a service.[205]

Many were quick to dismiss incidents like the one in Calgary because it didn't take place in the US, but similar attacks also happened in America. For example, California Governor Gavin Newsom, who faced and survived a recall election due to his COVID-19 tyranny, issued a blanket shutdown of indoor church services in the summer of 2020 and used armed police to enforce it.[206]

His orders were eventually overturned by the Supreme Court, but according to Justices Clarence Thomas, Neil Gorsuch, and Samuel Alito, religious liberty wasn't fully protected by the ruling.[207]

In New York City, Mayor Bill de Blasio threatened to permanently close churches and synagogues for not complying with his order to stop gathering during the COVID-19 outbreak. "If you go to your synagogue, if you go to your church and attempt to hold services after having been told so often not to, our enforcement agents will have no choice but to shut down those services," de Blasio said at a press conference at the time.[208]

There were also members of the family of believers who accepted and endorsed COVID-19 tyranny and oppression under a misguided and incorrect interpretation of Romans 13:1-5 (the infamously misused "submit to government authority" Scripture):

1. Let everyone be subject to the governing authorities, for there is no authority except that which God has established. The authorities that exist have been established by God.

2. Consequently, whoever rebels against the authority is rebelling against what God has instituted, and those who do so will bring judgment on themselves.

3. For rulers hold no terror for those who do right, but for those who do wrong. Do you want to be free from fear of the one in authority? Then do what is right and you will be commended.

4. For the one in authority is God's servant for your good. But if you do wrong, be afraid, for rulers do not bear the sword for no reason. They are God's servants, agents of wrath to bring punishment on the wrongdoer.

5. Therefore, it is necessary to submit to the authorities, not only because of possible punishment but also as a matter of conscience. (NIV)

Likewise, so-called Christians and/or so-called conservatives in the media with enormous national platforms not only surrendered to COVID-19 tyranny, but they also demonized Christians and conservatives who disagreed with them. Senior Editor of *The Dispatch* and columnist for *Time*, David French, called vaccine "hesitancy" a "spiritual problem," and he said that Christians who refused to wear a mask were not "pro-life."[209] And Editor-at-Large at *TheBulwark.com*, Bill Kristol, called conservatives who refused to wear a mask "nihilists."[210] (Nihilism is defined as "the rejection of all religious and moral principles, in the belief that life is meaningless.")[211]

"Christians" and "conservatives" who latched on to coronavirus hysteria did so to excuse their surrender to government tyranny and oppression and their submission to shutdowns, stay-at-home orders, and mask-wearing mandates. When they spewed nonsense about refusing to get vaccinated or refusing to wear a mask, they weren't motivated by liberty, they were motivated by guilt; the guilt they felt for bowing to government tyranny and oppression and the guilt they tried to inflict on others who refused to bow with them.

I cried foul on this mess before it was ever implemented, and I expected many of the liberty-killing consequences before they ever happened because I know the government has been a dismal failure when it comes to defending the Constitution.

CHAPTER 13

TYRANNY WINS, LIBERTY LOSES

"When all government, domestic and foreign, in little as in great things, shall be drawn to Washington as the center of all power, it will render powerless the checks provided of one government on another, and will become as venal and oppressive as the government from which we separated."[212]

THOMAS JEFFERSON

(Founding Father, third president of the United States, author of the Declaration of Independence)

"The accumulation of all powers, legislative, executive, and judiciary, in the same hands, whether of one, a few, or many, and whether hereditary, self-appointed, or elective, may justly be pronounced the very definition of tyranny."[213]

JAMES MADISON

(Founding Father, fourth president of the United States)

"In theory, Socialism may wish to enhance freedom, but in practice, every kind of collectivism consistently carried thought must produce the characteristic features which Fascism, Nazism, and Communism have in common."[214]

FRIEDRICH HAYEK

(Social theorist, political philosopher)

Washington made killing liberty standard operating procedure post-9/11, and COVID-19 helped take tyranny to the next level. Post-COVID-19, however, the government took the lessons learned from these so-called crises to build even more powerful ways to bring an end to freedom in America.

VACCINE PASSPORTS AND THE SOCIAL CREDIT SYSTEM

COVID-19 hysteria created the perfect opportunity to create digital vaccine passports, but hidden within their creation was this little tidbit: they used the same platform as the one created to build a totalitarian "social credit system" like the one used in communist China.[215] The Chinese social credit system is an all-encompassing regulatory system designed to report on the trustworthiness of individuals, corporations, and government entities across the country. Some of the areas tracked in real-time by China's "social credit system" are:

- ► Medical history
- ► Social media posts and internet search history
- ► Bank accounts and credit cards
- ► Residence, employment, and criminal history
- ► Relationships and religious activities
- ► Political activity[216]

This information gets fed to a central database to create a "social credit score" used to reward or punish citizens. Those with a high score are able to participate freely in society while those with a low score are prohibited from traveling, borrowing money, keeping a job, or even getting their children into school.[217]

Vaccine passports were allegedly designed to track COVID-19 compliance, but they could be used to launch a social credit system with little effort since they both use the same platform. If used to their full potential, vaccine passports could eventually lead to tracking and controlling every aspect of our lives.

GOVERNMENT POWER TO SPY ON YOUR MONEY

A little-known and often overlooked provision in the PATRIOT Act was a change made to the 1970 Bank Secrecy Act. Under the change, new standards were established for banks to identify customers and maintain records, requiring them to report cash transactions over $10,000.

Allegedly, this change was intended to prevent the funding of terrorist activities. In reality, it has resulted in a violation of the Fourth Amendment's protection against unreasonable search and seizure and the Fifth Amendment's guarantee of due process—proving that the government isn't just after power. It's after absolute power.

Early in Joe Biden's presidency, he introduced an "absolute power" program I refer to as a PATRIOT Act for the IRS. Under the original PATRIOT Act, the government's power to spy on our financial transactions was allegedly "limited," but Joe Biden's Patriot Act for the IRS expanded that power to allow Big Brother to spy on every one of your non-cash financial transactions.[218]

Biden claimed at the time that his plan to give the IRS power to spy on bank accounts would only target those labeled as rich, but it ultimately pulled in data on nearly every law-abiding, tax-compliant American because every bank and financial institution was required to participate.

DIGITAL CURRENCY AND A CASHLESS SOCIETY

After big government and big banks joined forces to create a digital currency capable of giving them the power to routinely and covertly manipulate how people spend their money, the news went out in 2023 about their launch of "digital wallets," a shift clearly intended to move us toward a cashless society.[219]

Contactless payments had become increasingly common during COVID-19, which gave the government new motivation to launch a cashless system run by Central Bank Digital Currencies (CBDCs). Of course, we were assured that a digital currency was necessary to "liberate" us from the constraints of greedy bankers and governments, and we were further assured that we would have unfettered access to our money.[220] What they didn't tell us, however, is how the state would be able to centrally harness our economic power and regulate it in ways that would mark the end of economic liberty.

The loss of privacy and liberty with CBDCs is obvious, an inconvenient truth that even the heads of the United States Federal Reserve and European Central Bank had to admit to at the time (via ReclaimTheNet.org):

> During an appearance at a Banque de France (Bank of France) event, the **chairman of the Federal Reserve, Jerome Powell**, said if the US were to pursue **a central bank digital currency** (CBDC), it **would be "identity verified" and "not anonymous."**

> "We would be looking to balance privacy protection with identity verification, which...has to be done, of course, in today's traditional banking system as well," Powell added.

> The **President of the European Central Bank (ECB), Christine Lagarde**, acknowledged that privacy was one of the main concerns Europeans had about the European Union's (EU's) proposed CBDC, the digital euro. Despite these concerns, she confirmed that **"there would not be complete anonymity** as there is with...bank notes" when using the digital euro.[221] (Emphasis mine)

Every individual and business loses their social and economic freedoms because digital dollars are traceable and programmable. Digital dollars can be created whenever the Federal Reserve chooses, with rules and restrictions built into their design, literally putting every single cent of our money under government control to be spent (or not spent) as Big Brother sees fit.

A digital dollar could, for example, be crafted to restrict fossil fuel use; it could also be used to enact de facto price controls by preventing you from spending more than the government thinks you should on particular products.

GOVERNMENT SPYING ON YOUR INTERNET USAGE

Always on the lookout for new ways to do things prohibited by the Constitution, government tyrants developed the "keyword warrant," a document that made it possible for them to spy on virtually everyone's internet activity without their knowledge.

In December 2020, we learned that the government spied on our internet use in 2019 by tracking our website visits using Section 215 of the PATRIOT Act.[222] This section is also where the NSA "found" its authority to gain access to "business records" and other "tangible things" deemed "relevant" to fighting terrorism, and using a broad interpretation of Section 215, the agency created its justification for the abusive and unconstitutional spying revealed by Edward Snowden.[223]

But the PATRIOT Act as written didn't provide the power the government needed to control every aspect of our lives, so a program that uses *keyword warrants* was created to get around the bulk data limitations of the PATRIOT Act, thus making it possible to spy on us—without our knowledge—whenever we use the internet.[224]

A keyword warrant is basically an open-ended request for information on anyone who searches the internet using particular terms. For example, instead of the government requesting all of arson suspect John Doe's Google searches, it requests information on all the people who searched Google for "arson."

The loss of liberty is obvious: In the first scenario, investigators have identified a suspect based on evidence presented to a judge, the typical standard for requesting a search warrant. In the second scenario, the government is demanding that search engines provide data to use for whatever reason they wish. This means, in practice, that someone who has done nothing illegal or wrong will be under government investigation based solely on that person's search engine history.

Think of everything you type into Google, Bing, or Yahoo. Keyword warrants allow unelected and unaccountable bureaucrats bent on destroying liberty to make decisions about your intentions based on what you've entered in a search bar. Keyword warrants are effectively fishing expeditions designed to make government spying easier while simultaneously avoiding that pesky Constitution.

INFRASTRUCTURE SPENDING AND GOVERNMENT SPYING

The bipartisan infrastructure bill signed into law by Joe Biden in 2021 included a provision to develop a system that makes it possible for the government to track every mile of every trip you take.[225] Within the 2,700 pages of the $1.2 trillion infrastructure bill—passed with the assistance of Republican frauds and liars who want you to believe they are the party of fiscal responsibility—is obscure language requiring the Department of Transportation to test the feasibility of taxing drivers for the number of miles they travel.

The brain trust behind this new tax was Secretary of Transportation Pete Buttigieg, who suggested adding it to the infrastructure bill, saying the idea showed "a lot of promise."[226] However, after receiving some backlash, Buttigieg reversed his stance a few days after suggesting it, and he assured America that a miles-driven tax would not be included in the legislation even though a pilot program to create such a tax was included in the legislation.[227]

The framework for a national surveillance system to track drivers has been under construction for several years. In January 2015, Obama and the Republican-controlled Congress passed legislation that allowed the US Drug Enforcement Agency (DEA) to create a national database of license plates and driving habits of

Americans.[228] Though originally created to combat drug trafficking, the program was later expanded to track other "criminals." This information was even made available to state-level law enforcement agencies.[229] This program's expansion was boosted in January 2018 when Trump and the Republican Party gave Immigration and Customs Enforcement (ICE) agency-wide access to a nationwide license plate recognition database to assist the agency with immigration control.[230]

In 2021, a bill known as the Stay Aware For Everyone (SAFE) Act (S.1406) was introduced that mandates driver-monitoring systems be installed in future cars.[231] Naturally, such a law opens up a can of worms where privacy is concerned, but sponsors of the bill (Sens. Richard Blumenthal, Ed Markey, and Amy Klobuchar) assured America that the Transportation Secretary would determine "appropriate privacy and data security safeguards."[232]

Years prior to the SAFE Act, Honda, Ford, General Motors, BMW, and Renault were already testing a radical new system that assigned digital IDs to individual autos linked to information such as ownership and service histories.[233] This data, covering the lifetime of the vehicle, would be used to recognize cars on the road, allowing the owner to pay fees automatically with no need for the specialized tags required in current electronic toll collection systems.

Talk about making Big Brother's job easier.

COVID TYRANNY: A BLUEPRINT FOR ADDRESSING CLIMATE CHANGE

In recent years at the time of this writing, our government overlords shredded the Constitution and implemented a plethora of COVID-19 lockdowns and mandates that some are saying could serve as a model to address the alleged threat posed by climate change.[234]

If you thought the government's abuse of power during COVID-19 was bad, wait until you see how using them to address climate change can make it worse (excerpts from Op-Ed by Kristin Tate via TheHill.com):

> The past two years have been a checklist for the worst impulses of government and public sentiment. COVID-19 allowed for supposedly **temporary measures to morph into two years of "emergency" restrictions.**
>
> **But what if COVID-19 was only the opening act, and another proclaimed crisis is the main event?** Implementing significant but partial restrictions, one by one, in the name of the common good can allow for encompassing government control that results in relatively little backlash. **Fear over climate change could lead to long-term soft lockdowns, given the precedent of immense growth of government power and significant support for sweeping state actions.**

This isn't a right-wing fever dream. Calls for harsh government measures in the name of saving the environment are already in the parlance of influential organizations and figures.

In November 2020, the Red Cross proclaimed that **climate change is a bigger threat than COVID-19 and should be confronted with "the same urgency."** Bill Gates recently demanded dramatic measures to prevent climate change, claiming it will be worse than the pandemic. Despite millions of people having died from COVID-19, **former governor of the Bank of England Mark Carney last year predicted that climate deaths will dwarf those of the pandemic.**

Lockdowns, which significantly reduced carbon emissions during 2020, could be the solution.[235] (Emphasis mine)

In March 2021, a report published by a group of climate scientists documented how carbon emissions fell thanks to COVID-19 lockdowns and how, in order to meet goals spelled out in the Paris Climate Agreement, government-mandated lockdowns could be used once every two years to end global warming and keep the earth at "safe" temperature levels.[236] Such a scenario could easily become a reality using the well-established abuse of executive power we've witnessed from the White House over the past several presidencies.

For example, far-left Democrats have suggested continuing the tradition of Donald Trump's routine abuse of executive power to address climate change.[237] In an appearance on CBS's *Face the Nation* during the 2020 election season, Washington Governor Jay Inslee (D)—he was running against Biden at the time for the Democrat nomination for president—was asked about Trump's emergency declaration for border security. In response, Inslee warned Republicans that Trump's abuse of executive power would greenlight a new standard by which Democrats would govern on issues like so-called climate change.

> Republicans ought to stand up on their hind legs, because they took an oath to the Constitution, not to Donald Trump, and reverse this decision … But if there are new rules, the Republicans have to understand that Democrats will play by whatever the rules are, particularly when it comes to climate change.[238]

In an interview with Rachel Maddow shortly after becoming Senate Majority Leader in 2020, Chuck Schumer also used Trump's track record of abuse of executive power to suggest that Biden do the same thing to declare a state of emergency to address climate change:

It might be a **good idea for President Biden to call a climate emergency...He can do many, many things under the emergency powers...** that he could do without legislation...Trump used this emergency [power] for a stupid wall, which wasn't an emergency. **But if there ever was an emergency, climate is one**.[239] (Emphasis mine)

Sen. Marco Rubio essentially predicted that Trump's abuse of executive power when he declared his border a "national emergency" could greenlight Biden to do the same in the name of fighting climate change.[240] In a January 2019 CNBC interview, the Florida Republican issued the following warning:

We have to be careful about endorsing broad uses of executive power...If today, the national emergency is border security... tomorrow, the national emergency might be climate change.[241]

Of course, Rubio and the rest of the spineless Republican Party did nothing to stop Trump's abuse of executive power, but you can easily replace the words "border security" with "COVID-19" and come to the same conclusion.

COVID TYRANNY: A BLUEPRINT FOR VOIDING THE SECOND AMENDMENT

Using his own unconstitutional abuse of power to address COVID-19 as an example, NY Governor Andrew Cuomo declared that gun violence was a pandemic in July 2021, prompting him to issue a statewide "disaster emergency" aimed at cracking down on gun ownership.[242] The disaster emergency order was the first of its kind in the country at the time, and it allowed the state to quickly allocate money and other resources to areas of New York where gun violence was running rampant, according to Cuomo.

The new disaster emergency on gun violence was issued just days after Cuomo's disaster emergency on COVID-19 expired, and he equated gun violence with the so-called pandemic worthy of being treated as a public health crisis. "If you can beat COVID-19, you can beat gun violence," the governor said.[243] "We're in a new epidemic, and it's gun violence, and it's a matter of life and death also."

Even before COVID-19, however, calls to use executive power to dismantle the Second Amendment were underway at the federal level. On the one-year anniversary of the mass shooting at Marjory Stoneman Douglas High School in Florida, Nancy Pelosi—she was Speaker of the House at the time—informed her Republican colleagues that based on Trump's example, a Democrat president could use a national emergency to impose unconstitutional gun control.[244]

A Democratic president can declare emergencies as well ... So the precedent that [Trump] is setting here is something that should be met with great unease and dismay by the Republicans. Let's talk about ... the one-year anniversary of another manifestation of the epidemic of gun violence in America. That's a national emergency. Why don't you declare that emergency, Mr. President? I wish you would.

In support of Pelosi's demands, Rep. Emanuel Cleaver posted a list of issues on social media that he thought needed to be addressed using a "national emergency" declaration:

► Gun violence is a national emergency;
► Climate change is a national emergency;
► Income inequality is a national emergency;
► Access to healthcare is a national emergency;
► Building a wall on the southern border is not.[245]

When it comes to the assault on our constitutional rights and the future of liberty, government tyrants rarely launch a full-blown frontal attack because their intentions would be too obvious. Instead, the strategy most often used is one that mirrors the advice senior demon Screwtape gave his nephew Wormwood in the CS Lewis satirical novel, *The Screwtape Letters*: "Indeed, the safest road to hell is the gradual one, the gentle slope, soft underfoot, without sudden turnings, without milestones, without signposts."[246]

CHAPTER 14

POLICE STATE AND THE END OF THE BILL OF RIGHTS

"Once a government is committed to the principle of silencing the voice of opposition, it has only one way to go, and that is down the path of increasingly repressive measures, until it becomes a source of terror to all its citizens and creates a country where everyone lives in fear."[247]

HARRY S. TRUMAN
(33rd president of the United States)

"The concept that the Bill of Rights and other constitutional protections against arbitrary government are inoperative when they become inconvenient or when expediency dictates otherwise is a very dangerous doctrine and if allowed to flourish would destroy the benefit of a written Constitution and undermine the basis of our government."[248]

JUSTICE HUGO BLACK
(Associate justice of the United States Supreme Court)

"The definition of a police state is when the government's prime concern is for its own safety, not for the lives, liberty, and property of the people it has sworn to protect."[249]

ANDREW NAPOLITANO
(New Jersey Superior Court justice, syndicated columnist)

139

George W. Bush. Barack Hussein Obama. Donald J. Trump. Joseph R. Biden. These are the names of the four men who occupied the White House following 9/11 and who facilitated the rise of the new Axis of Evil that gave birth to the police state America has lived under since that dreadful day. Tyranny has truly been a bipartisan affair between Republicans and Democrats.[250]

George W. Bush got the ball rolling in the days following the 9/11 terrorist attacks when the man who once "abandoned free market principles to save the free market system" showed us that he was also willing to abandon the principles of liberty and freedom to allegedly save liberty and freedom. Bush joined forces with a unanimous Congress to create a myriad of agencies and programs responsible for killing liberty.

The TSA. The Patriot Act. The Patriot Act II. Warrantless spying on Americans by the NSA under the "President's Surveillance Program." These are just a few of the ways George W. Bush helped build the police state, proving that "compassionate conservative" was really code for "passive progressive," and provided a foundation for Barack Obama to build upon.

During his presidency, we learned that Obama expanded warrantless NSA spying on the phones and computers of Americans—thank you, Edward Snowden—an expansion he defended because it was "transparent" while providing "security" without sacrificing "our freedom."[251] Obama's expansion of NSA power came as no surprise to those paying attention. On July 2, 2008, then-candidate Obama made this promise during a Boulder, Colorado, campaign stop:

> We cannot continue to rely on our military in order to achieve the national security objectives we've set. We've got to have a **civilian national security force** that's just as powerful, just as strong, just as well-funded.[252] (Emphasis mine)

While this promise was quickly forgotten after he became president, Obama appeared to put some muscle behind his words when he ordered his Department of Homeland Security (DHS) to buy billions of rounds of ammunition—enough to empty five rounds into the body of every American living at the time.

Obama was also the man who began the militarization of local police forces. He authorized the purchase of military equipment, as well as instituting a DOJ plan to federalize local police. Under Obama, we also witnessed how the NSA and local police were using fake cell phone towers to spy on Americans.

Just days after his inauguration, Donald Trump indicated that he was ready to pick up where his predecessor left off with the federalization of local police. Right out of the gate, he threatened to "send in the Feds" if the City of Chicago failed to address their violence problem in a manner to his liking.[253] In October 2019, Trump made preparations to do just that when he spoke at the International Association of Chiefs of Police in Chicago. In his speech, Trump announced a plan to begin a sweeping crackdown on crime using a program he referred to as "the surge."[254] Sen. Ron Paul called the plan "the Patriot Act on steroids."[255]

Though initially delayed, Trump used COVID-19 hysteria, Black Lives Matter riots, and his collapsing 2020 reelection campaign to make good on his tyrannical police state ambitions. His DOJ ordered the DHS to begin "the surge" in Portland, Oregon. Federal agents, dressed in fatigues and wearing no badges or Federal ID, abducted protesters, hauled them off to detention centers in unmarked vans, and conducted intelligence gathering as instructed by the DOJ.

This Gestapo-styled attack on liberty pleased Trump so much so that he promised to send his federalized police force to "other cities to deal with unrest"—a threat he made good on when he sent them to Chicago and Albuquerque.[256] Tom Ridge, the first DHS Secretary, said at the time that Trump's actions had turned the Department into "the president's personal militia," a sentiment also shared by Judge Andrew Napolitano, who called Trump's police state actions "unconstitutional."[257, 258]

Throughout Trump's presidency, the NSA continued to spy at will, enabling the agency to collect massive amounts of call data on Americans. Trump was also instrumental in the expansion of FISA702, and he attempted to expand and make permanent the NSA's spying programs.[259]

This brings us to Joe Biden, who used America's growing comfort with government tyranny to dismantle the Bill of Rights and continue to build a police state. Early in the first year of his presidency, Biden unveiled his National Strategy for Countering Domestic Terrorism to counter the rise in "domestic terrorism"—a phrase he used to describe people critical of a tyrannical government—to add thousands of prosecutors and other law enforcement officials to the government payroll, including new personnel in the DOJ and the Department of Homeland Security.[260] He also created a Big Brother-styled monitoring system to track federal and non-federal employees deemed by the government to be an "inside threat."[261]

In August 2021, Biden's DHS issued a terrorism threat advisory designed to silence the dissenting voices of people exercising their God-given, constitutionally protected right to free speech to protest and criticize the government. The advisory defined "terrorists" as pushers of "anti-government rhetoric" who stood in "opposition to COVID-19 measures."[262]

Biden also leveraged COVID-19 hysteria into an opportunity to address so-called misinformation on the subjects of vaccines and mask mandates by turning Big Tech companies into de facto speech police by requiring them to surrender to the federal government the user data of people found to be spreading such misinformation.[263] Biden also introduced the idea of creating an Orwellian Ministry of Truth with the Misinformation/Disinformation Board.[264]

In October 2021, Biden's DOJ labeled parents concerned about Critical Race Theory being taught in public schools "domestic terrorists" when Attorney General Merrick Garland issued a memorandum about the "disturbing spike in harassment, intimidation, and threats of violence against school administrators, board members, teachers, and staff."[265]

In 2022, Joe Biden began to literally build a police state when he created a unit within the DOJ to deal specifically with domestic terrorism as defined by the administration.

Another target of Biden's domestic terrorism agenda was the Second Amendment. Biden secretly built a national gun registry.[266] Credit card companies helped by tracking the gun and ammunition purchases of their customers and making those records available to the feds.[267]

This is just a snapshot of the myriad of ways George W. Bush, Barack Hussein Obama, Donald J. Trump, and Joseph R. Biden were of one mind when it came to building a police state capable of destroying the Bill of Rights. We can reclaim the liberty these men destroyed, but only when we get rid of the tyrannical Republican/Democrat duopoly and replace them with patriots who will work *within* the Constitution and not *around* it.

CHAPTER 15

COMPROMISE AND THE CULTURAL COLLAPSE OF SOCIETY

*"There will be, in the next generation or so, a
pharmacological method of making people
love their servitude and producing dictatorship
without tears, so to speak, producing a kind of
painless concentration camp for entire societies,
so that people will in fact have their liberties taken
away from them, but will rather enjoy it."[268]*

ALDOUS HUXLEY
(English writer and philosopher)

*"The essential feature of government is the
enforcement of its decrees by beating, killing,
and imprisoning. Those who are asking for more
government interference are asking ultimately
for more compulsion and less freedom."[269]*

LUDWIG VON MISES
(Economist, historian, sociologist)

*"If we ever forget that we are One Nation Under
God, then we will be a nation gone under."[270]*

RONALD REAGAN
(40th president of the United States)

T he late great Andrew Breitbart, the conservative activist and founder of *Breitbart News*, held firmly to the belief that "Politics is downstream from culture," and he used this idea to build a platform to battle the left-leaning cultural bias prevalent in Hollywood and the media.[271] As a conservative, Andrew was also making the point that politics is a reflection of cultural beliefs and that conservatives were losing the political battle because they were unwilling to be soldiers in the culture war waged by LGBT extremists. Meanwhile, the Left was not only fighting this culture war, they had already decided they weren't taking prisoners.

EXHIBIT A: MASTERPIECE CAKESHOP V. COLORADO CIVIL RIGHTS COMMISSION

In a narrow 7-2 decision in June 2018, the Supreme Court ruled in favor of Jack Phillips, a Christian baker who refused to bake a custom wedding cake for a homosexual couple based on the grounds that doing so would violate his religious liberty.[272] How is a 7-2 ruling a narrow decision? Because even though Mr. Phillips was the victor in a lopsided vote total, the root issue concerning his case (Freedom of Religion) was left unanswered. The court's decision wasn't so much pro-First Amendment as it was anti-Colorado Civil Rights Commission. Writing for the majority, Anthony Kennedy, the Justice responsible for constitutionalizing same-sex marriage, confirmed this fact when he noted that the case created a "difficult situation" when it came to how the LGBT agenda impacted religious liberty along with his belief that the issue "must await further elaboration" in the courts.[273]

While people like Franklin Graham, the Evangelical who winked at Donald Trump's sexual indiscretions because he was "chosen by God's hand," proclaimed the Masterpiece Cakeshop decision a "huge win for religious freedom" and served as proof that God answers prayer, the reality was that religious liberty was no safer after the decision than it was before it.[274, 275]

In his analysis of the Supreme Court ruling, Daniel Horowitz, Sr. Editor at *Conservative Review* who specializes in judicial matters, used his X (formerly known as Twitter) account to point out how the decision fell short of protecting religious liberty because the Court never addressed whether the state or federal government had the power to make laws forcing individuals to violate their consciences.

> Folks, this opinion is insanely narrow and the fight against religious liberty and the codification of rainbow jihad as the religion of the land has only begun. We need legislation pushing back. Yes, it could have been worse, but this is hardly [a] reason to celebrate...It's very clear at least 5 justices believe a state can order you to violate your conscience with your own private business in most cases.[276]

THE NEW AXIS OF EVIL

The ACLU, who represented the plaintiffs in the case, was pleased with the Court's decision, saying that it was,

> . . . based on concerns unique to the [Masterpiece Cakeshop] case but that it reaffirmed its long-standing rule that states can prevent the harms of discrimination in the marketplace, including against LGBT people.[277]

Translation? According to the ACLU, the Court affirmed the right for states to pass laws forcing businesses to serve anyone, anytime, anyplace for any reason—First Amendment be damned.

This case served as an example of how we are edging ever closer to becoming a post-constitutional America where judicial tyranny replaces the checks and balances provided by three separate but equal branches of government. While Masterpiece Cakeshop won this case, the ruling could have just as easily gone the other way with a different set of judges hearing the same evidence.

COLORADO STRIKES AGAIN!

As I and other conservatives warned following the *Masterpiece Cakeshop v. Colorado Civil Rights Commission* ruling, the Supreme Court's failure to protect religious liberty meant the government could still pass laws forcing

Christians to violate their consciences in the marketplace. These warnings proved to be prophetic mere weeks later when Autumn Scardina, a man who identifies as a transgender woman, and the Colorado Civil Rights Commission joined forces to file another lawsuit against Jack Phillips, this time for refusing to bake a pink cake with blue frosting celebrating Scardina's gender transition.

Following a lower Colorado court ruling against Phillips, a Colorado Court of Appeals three-judge panel, all appointed by Democrat governors, ruled unanimously in January 2023 in favor of the LGBT agenda and against religious liberty when they agreed with Scardina's claim that Phillips and his Masterpiece Cakeshop were guilty of transgender discrimination by declining to bake the cake.[278] Scardina said during the March 2021 trial held by the lower court that the attempt to order the cake was a test to see whether Phillips would make good on his assertion that he would sell any other type of product but opposed making a gay couple's wedding cake because, as a Christian, he was opposed to the religious ceremony involved, according to a CBS Denver report.[279]

Being forced to bake a cake celebrating a same-sex wedding or gender transition is small potatoes compared to what has happened to religious liberty since these decisions. This was confirmed by Douglas Laycock, a pro-LGBT law professor at the University of Virginia and a proponent of federal gay-rights non-discrimination laws back in 2019, when he said that laws like the Equality Act were designed to "crush" religious dissenters.[280]

Trump, Republicans in the Senate, and so-called conservative groups pretend to oppose actions like those taken by the Colorado Civil Rights Commission, but they do so primarily to stir up the base during election cycles. Their track record shows how they readily abandon their opposition after the election. For example, in his acceptance speech at the 2016 Republican National Convention, Trump promised to "do everything in [his] power to protect LGBTQ citizens," a promise he acted upon immediately after he was sworn in.[281] On the advice of his daughter Ivanka and her husband Jared Kushner, Trump let an Obama executive order stand that was purportedly issued to protect LGBT employees of government contractors.[282]

After Ivanka and Jared convinced Daddy to leave Obama's executive order alone, Mike Pence—I believe the "P" in his name should stand for "Pusillanimous"—defended this decision in an interview and bragged about his support of Trump's embrace of the pro-LGBT agenda.

I think throughout the campaign, President Trump made it clear that discrimination would have no place in our administration. I mean, he was the very first Republican nominee to mention the LGBTQ community at our Republican National Convention and was applauded for it ... And I was there applauding with him.[283]

Pence's spineless defense isn't much of a surprise when we remember that the so-called "Christian conservative" caved to LGBT extremists as governor of Indiana when he personally dismantled that state's version of the Religious Freedom Restoration Act.[284]

During the 2020 presidential campaign season, Trump openly supported Democrat Pete Buttigieg's appearance on stage with his "husband." In a FOX News interview where he was asked about it, Trump responded, "I think that's something that perhaps some people will have a problem with. I have no problem with it whatsoever. I think it's good."[285]

Christian conservatives have been missing in action in the culture war because they have embraced immorality and socialism as a part of their "Christian" faith ever since the Fellowship of the Pharisees abandoned the Gospel of Jesus Christ to support Donald Trump in 2016, much like the 1930s church supported Hitler. Unfortunately, their defense of Trump's indefensible behavior continued during his 2020 reelection campaign. Even after seeing every warning about Trump's unethical and immoral behavior come to pass, these false prophets and heretics continued giving him their unconditional support, destroying faith and American culture in the process.[286] To summarize the fallout from these facts: who cares what "leaders" like Franklin Graham or Robert Jeffress have to say about the evils of the LGBT agenda when they hypocritically defend the immoral behavior of Donald Trump?

Compromising Christian constitutional conservative values ends with the destruction of our culture and our society . . . all because faux conservatives and Evangelicals are too cowardly and/or lukewarm to fight for them.

CHAPTER 16

THE END OF NATIONAL SOVEREIGNTY

"Some even believe we (the Rockefeller family) are part of a secret cabal working against the best interests of the United States, characterizing my family and me as 'internationalists' and of conspiring with others around the world to build a more integrated global political and economic structure—one world, if you will. If that's the charge, I stand guilty, and I am proud of it."[287]

DAVID ROCKEFELLER
(Banker, philanthropist)

"The one thing man fears is the unknown. When presented with this scenario, individual rights will be willingly relinquished for the guarantee of their well-being granted to them by a World Government, a New World Order."[288]

HENRY KISSINGER
(Secretary of State and National Security Advisor for Presidents Richard Nixon and Gerald Ford)

"COVID-19 has reminded us that the biggest problems we face are global in nature. Whether it's pandemics, climate change, terrorism or international trade, all are global issues that we can only address, and whose risks can only be mitigated, in a collective fashion."[289]

KLAUS SCHWAB
(Founder of the World Economic Forum)

F rom 9/11 to the COVID-19 pandemic, the Axis of Evil's prevailing solutions to various crises always came down on the side of tyranny and the loss of liberty; in other words, the end of the America envisioned and created by the Founding Fathers and the end of national sovereignty.

In an address to the American people following the 1991 invasion of Kuwait by Iraq, President George H.W. Bush announced the launch of "Operation Desert Storm," a plan where, in his words, "a new world order can emerge."[290] What is the new world order? It is the utopian goal of creating a one-world government to rule over the entire globe.[291] And while this goal remained in the shadows of foreign affairs for years after Bush first mentioned it, the terrorist attacks of 9/11 and the COVID-19 pandemic gave tyrants bent on destroying our constitutional republic the fuel it needed to ignite the blaze that would burn our national sovereignty to the ground.

When COVID-19 first hit the national stage, Henry Kissinger, the former national security advisor and secretary of state for Presidents Richard Nixon and Gerald Ford, insisted that the United States would have to join a global program to repair the damage wrought by the pandemic, and said that, "Failure to do so could set the world on fire."[292] He also demanded "a global collaborative vision and program" along with an adherence to the "principles of the liberal world order."[293]

According to Antony P. Mueller, a German professor of economics and contributor to the *Mises Wire* (published by the Mises Institute), nefarious globalists had long planned on using something like COVID-19 to launch the New World Order, taking us from lockdowns to "The Great Reset."[294] To form this New World Order, global policymakers began advocating for a "Great Reset" with the intent of creating a global technocracy that would require close cooperation between the heads of the digital industry—people like Bill Gates—and governments.[295] With programs such as guaranteed minimum income and healthcare for all rising from the ashes of COVID-19, this new kind of governance combines strict societal control with the promise of comprehensive social justice.

This overhaul of the world envisioned by the Great Reset is the brainchild of an elite group of businessmen and politicians known as the World Economic Forum (WEF) and its leader, Klaus Schwab. In a 2020 announcement, Schwab provided a preview of the 2121 WEF meeting where he had this to say about it:

A Great Reset is necessary to build a new social contract that honors the dignity of every human being. The global health crisis has laid bare the unsustainability of our old system in terms of social cohesion, the lack of equal opportunities and inclusiveness. Nor can we turn our backs on the evils of racism and discrimination. We need to build into this new social contract our intergenerational responsibility to ensure that we live up to the expectations of young people.

COVID-19 has accelerated our transition into the age of the Fourth Industrial Revolution. We have to make sure that the new technologies in the digital, biological and physical world remain human-centered and serve society as a whole, providing everyone with fair access.

This global pandemic has also demonstrated again how interconnected we are. We have to restore a functioning system of smart global cooperation structured to address the challenges of the next 50 years. The Great Reset will require us to integrate all stakeholders of global society into a community of common interest, purpose and action. We need a change of mindset, moving from short-term to long-term thinking, moving from shareholder capitalism to stakeholder responsibility. Environmental, social and good governance have to be a measured part of corporate and governmental accountability.[296]

DONALD TRUMP'S CONNECTION TO THE GREAT RESET

Donald Trump's "Make America Great Again" rhetoric is connected to the Great Reset through his daughter and former advisor, Ivanka (via White House archives):

> Ivanka Trump is Advisor to the President. In her role, she focuses on the education and economic empowerment of women and their families as well as job creation and economic growth through workforce development, skills training and entrepreneurship.

> Prior to her father's election as the forty-fifth President of the United States, Ivanka oversaw development and acquisitions at the Trump Organization alongside her brothers Donald Jr. and Eric. Ivanka led some of the company's largest and most complex transactions.

> Also an entrepreneur, Ivanka founded an eponymous lifestyle brand.

> Ivanka graduated from the Wharton School of Business at the University of Pennsylvania in 2004.

> Ivanka is the author of two New York Times and Wall Street Journal bestselling books.

> Ivanka has been included in Fortune magazine's prestigious "40 Under 40" list (2014) and was

honored as a Young Global Leader by the World Economic Forum (2015). Most recently, Ivanka was also featured in Time's 100 Most Influential list (2017) and Forbes' "World's 100 Most Powerful Women" (2017).[297]

Klaus Schwab is the founder of Young Global Leaders, a program designed to train globalist puppets to become leaders and people of influence in the New World Order. Any doubts about this were eliminated by the man himself in a 2017 appearance at the John F. Kennedy School of Government when he bragged about how he used his handpicked leaders of tomorrow to "penetrate governments" and reshape the world in his image:

And I have to say, when I mention our names, like Mrs. Merkel, even Vladimir Putin, and so on, they all have been young global leaders of the World Economic Forum.

But what we are very proud of now is the young generation like Prime Minister Trudeau, president of Argentina and so on . . . So, we penetrate the cabinets.[298]

In 2018, Donald Trump appeared at the WEF held in Davos and declared that his nationalist "America First" agenda would be instrumental in building a New World Order through the Great Reset.

America First does not mean America alone . . .
I am here today to represent the interests of the
American People and to **affirm America's friend-
ship and partnership in building a better world**.
Like all nations represented at this forum, America
hopes for a future in which everyone can prosper
and every child can grow up free from violence,
poverty, and fear.[299] (Emphasis mine)

In 2020, Trump spoke at the 50th anniversary of the
WEF—the Great Reset was the theme again that year—and
began his time on stage with what he described as "The
Great American Comeback" before repeating many of the
talking points he gave two years earlier.[300]

JOE BIDEN GOES ALL-IN ON THE GREAT RESET AND THE NEW WORLD ORDER

Immediately after he won the 2020 election, Joe Biden appointed John Kerry to be his "Climate Czar" who, as the official representative of the new administration, spoke at
a panel discussion hosted by the WEF where he revealed
his new boss' devotion to the New World Order and the
Great Reset.[301]

Here is just a sampling of Kerry's comments:

The answer to your question is, no, you're not expecting too much [from President Biden]. And yes, [the Great Reset] will happen. And I think **it will happen with greater speed and with greater intensity** than a lot of people might imagine ... [The need for the Great Reset is] **a reflection of the inability of democratic governments in many parts of the world to deliver.** And I just have to put it bluntly. We're certainly the primary exhibit. **We're exhibit number one** ... I think ... that the notion of a 'reset' is more important than ever before. I personally believe that we're at the dawn of an extremely exciting time.[302] (Emphasis mine)

According to the WEF, climate change requires that we "decarbonize the economy" (via the Green New Deal) and bring human thinking and behavior "into harmony with nature" through the urgent implementation of the Great Reset.[303]

In 2022, Biden gave an address at the Business Roundtable and called on America to lead in creating a "New World Order" to "unite the world," an idea he has supported ever since his buddy President George H.W. Bush first uttered the words on January 16, 1991 (via EagleObserver.com):

On April 23, 1992, Biden, then chairman of the Senate Foreign Relations Committee's European Affairs Subcommittee, published a piece in the Wall Street

Journal, **"How I Learned to Love the New World Order."** In it he expressed a need for a "permanent commitment of forces for use by the Security Council"–a U.N. standing army–adding, "Why not breathe life into the U.N. Charter?" **His plans would destroy national sovereignty and establish world government over all nations under the United Nations.**

This was no fluke position. In a speech as vice president to the Export-Import Bank conference in Washington D.C. on April 5, 2013, he reiterated that theme. **"The affirmative task we have now is to, um, create a new world order, because the global order is changing again.**

The next year he told graduating cadets of the U.S. Air Force Academy Class of 2014, **"You, your class, has an incredible window of opportunity to lead in shaping a new world order for the 21st century."**[304] (Emphasis mine)

Bush believed his vision for a New World Order would "succeed" if managed by a "credible United Nations" that used its "peacekeeping role" to fulfill the vision of the organization's founders.[305] Looking back on the years and the multitude of crises (both real and manufactured) that have passed since then, it's looking more likely that Bush's dream will be realized at the cost of America's sovereignty and liberty.

A TIME FOR CHOOSING

"Two roads diverged in a yellow wood,
And sorry I could not travel both
And be one traveler, long I stood
And looked down one as far as I could
To where it bent in the undergrowth;

Then took the other, as just as fair,
And having perhaps the better claim,
Because it was grassy and wanted wear;
Though as for that the passing there
Had worn them really about the same,

And both that morning equally lay
In leaves no step had trodden black.
Oh, I kept the first for another day!

CHAPTER 17

CHOOSE TO BREAK FREE OF THE MATRIX

"The highest courage is to dare to be yourself in the face of adversity. Choosing right over wrong, ethics over convenience, and truth over popularity...these are the choices that measure your life. Travel the path of integrity without looking back, for there is never a wrong time to do the right thing."

UNKNOWN

"In any moment of decision, the best thing you can do is the right thing. The worst thing you can do is nothing."[307]

THEODORE ROOSEVELT

(26th president of the United States)

"Never do anything against conscience even if the state demands it."[308]

ALBERT EINSTEIN

(German physicist)

"I was not born to be forced. I will breathe after my own fashion. Let us see who is the strongest."[309]

HENRY DAVID THOREAU

(Naturalist, poet, philosopher)

I n the 1999 movie *The Matrix*, Thomas Anderson, a computer programmer who later became known as Neo, lives a boring and frustrated life. By day, Anderson works his 9-5 programmer job, but by night, he's a hacker who sells his services on the black market. Thanks to a mysterious woman named Trinity, Neo learns that his life has been an elaborate deception created by an all-controlling evil cyber-intelligence.

After meeting with a man named Morpheus, Neo decides to join in a rebellion against the machine world that created the Matrix and the agents, led by a program known as Mr. Smith, responsible for keeping humanity trapped inside a false reality known only as the Matrix.

Throughout the movie, we examine concepts like: What is real? Who are we meant to be? How do we reclaim our freedom?

When it comes to breaking free of the Washington "Matrix," each of us must choose to do so if we are to have any chance of defeating the Republican/Democrat machine. I've made it my life's work to expose the many ways liberty is being destroyed by the "agents" represented by the Republican and Democrat parties. I've also exposed the faux conservatives in Washington and the media who have replaced conviction with capitulation.

This has led to some amazing criticism from people who don't agree with my conclusions. Some of the most common accusations (besides being accused of working for CNN or being privately funded by George Soros) are how my behavior is negative and un-Christian, and how I should focus more on the "good things" done by so-called conservatives. Of course, I'd be happy to do as they suggest if they actually did anything good. Unfortunately, Trumpism and nationalism have blurred the lines of conservatism to such an extent that it's nearly impossible to find anything "good" to praise.

The Washington Matrix is an evil and oppressive system built for only one purpose: the creation of a dystopian society designed to keep us trapped inside a simulated world where the machine is in control and where we are relegated to being little more than an energy source used to sustain it.

I've been fighting the Washington Matrix ever since Agents John Boehner and Mitch McConnell teamed up with like-minded Republicans—and Democrats—to "crush" the freed minds of the conservative movement. I continue to fight the wave of fascism and nationalism being embraced by Republicans and the wave of socialism and Marxism being embraced by Democrats.

So-called conservative groups like the House Freedom Caucus (HFC), whose members at one time had freed themselves of the Washington Matrix, have negotiated their way back into the system. Now, instead of fighting the Washington Matrix, the HFC and others are content to work with the agents to help them advance Trumpism and nationalism.

And let's not forget that Trump has become the "Mr. Smith" of agents, targeting freed conservative minds and forcing them to either allow themselves to be re-assimilated into the Washington Matrix or be destroyed.

To put it bluntly, I'm now part of the resistance. My mind has been freed from the programming of the Washington Matrix, and I'm committed to doing all I can to free as many other minds as possible. I'm a critic of the system, not a cheerleader, because truth is more important than going along to get along within a system designed to control my life. I often find myself alone, but as I once wrote, "I'd rather walk the right road alone than walk the wrong road with a crowd."[310]

When faced with the overwhelming forces of the Washington Matrix and their war against the conservative values of freed minds, I'm often reminded of a scene near the end of the movie, *The Matrix Revolutions*, the third installment of The Matrix trilogy, where Agent Smith appears to have defeated Neo.

Agent Smith: Why, Mr. Anderson? Why do you do it? Why get up? Why keep fighting? Do you believe you're fighting for something? For more than your survival? Can you tell me what it is? Do you even know? Is it freedom? Or truth? Perhaps peace? Yes? No? Could it be for love? Illusions, Mr. Anderson. Vagaries of perception. The temporary constructs of a feeble human intellect trying desperately to justify an existence that is without meaning or purpose. And all of them as artificial as the Matrix itself, although only a human mind could invent something as insipid as love. You must be able to see it, Mr. Anderson. You must know it by now. You can't win. It's pointless to keep fighting. Why, Mr. Anderson? Why? Why do you persist?

Neo: Because I choose to.[311]

"Because I choose to." That's it right there. Liberty or tyranny. Freedom or slavery. Surrender or revolution. To break free of the Washington Matrix, we need to choose to fight for what we believe in.

I choose to be a member of the resistance who speaks the truth because, as George Orwell has been credited as saying, "Speaking the truth in times of universal deceit is a revolutionary act."[312] And regardless of the outcome, I will continue doing all I can to be "The One" who helps break the grip the Washington Matrix has over us, and I will continue fighting the agents—including the faux conservatives in Washington and the media—whenever freed conservative minds are under assault.

In *The Matrix*, another character exists known as the Oracle, a program from the Machine world initially created to interpret the reasons humans do what they do. Her insight into human behavior was so strong that she developed an almost spiritual ability to shape events. She eventually leaves the Machine world and goes into exile inside the Matrix to aid The Resistance against the Machines.

The Washington Matrix has its own "Oracles"—I refer to them as the Fellowship of the Pharisees—and I choose to call them out for their spiritual capitulation and sacrificing the Gospel of Jesus Christ on the altar of cheap grace for a seat at the table of political power.

How about you? Will you choose to remain in the bondage of the Washington Matrix? Or will you choose to break free of it, accepting the life of liberty we were meant to live?

Like Neo, I chose the latter, and I hope you will too!

CHAPTER 18

CHOOSE TO ABANDON THE REPUBLICAN/ DEMOCRAT DUOPOLY

"Saying we should keep the two-party system simply because it is working is like saying the Titanic voyage was a success because a few people survived on life-rafts."[313]

EUGENE MCCARTHY
(Writer, congressman)

"There is nothing I dread so much as the division of the republic into two great parties, each arranged under its leader, and concerting measures in opposition to each other. This, in my humble apprehension, is to be dreaded as the greatest political evil under our constitution."[314]

JOHN ADAMS
(Founding Father, second president of the United States)

"In their moral justification, the argument of the lesser evil has played a prominent role. If you are confronted with two evils, the argument runs, it is your duty to opt for the lesser one, whereas it is irresponsible to refuse to choose altogether. Its weakness has always been that those who choose the lesser evil forget quickly that they chose evil."[315]

HANNAH ARENDT
(German historian, philosopher)

U nder the so-called two-party system, every election, particularly presidential elections, typically boils down to a vote between a "tomayto" and a "tomahto." They're both the same kind of fruit; the only difference is in how you pronounce their name. The consequences of continuing to play the game built by the Republican/ Democrat duopoly for the benefit of the Republican/ Democrat duopoly are so grave that if we continue to participate, we do so at our own peril. Quite simply, the days of binary voting (Republican or Democrat) simply because the other side is worse need to end . . . starting right now! The Democratic Party is filled with leftist radicals pretending to be moderate, while the Republican Party is filled with a bunch of sniveling, spineless, leftist cowards pretending to be conservatives. Republicans are quick to unfurl the banner of conservatism every two years during an election, but they just as quickly fold it up and store it away once their campaign coffers are full and their votes secured. To them, being a conservative is a matter of convenience, not conviction. To put it bluntly, conservatives no longer have a home within the GOP.

As a movement, conservatives have been all too willing to accept the crumbs falling from the GOP establishment's table even as we convinced ourselves that having an "R" in office was better than having a "D." Unfortunately, this binary approach to voting has done more harm than good to our conservative values. Party bosses—or perhaps thugs would be a more appropriate description–demand our capitulation to their self-interested agenda under the threat of retribution if we choose not to toe the party line.

Despite their oft-repeated promise to be a firewall against socialism, the Republican Party has adopted much of the far left's socialist agenda to create a rebranded conservative agenda known as nationalism, which has become the identity of the Republican Party. It's important to remember that when we say the "far-left," we aren't only talking about Democrats anymore. The far-left now describes everyone not considered a conservative. For example: Republican Mitch McConnell was no different than Democrat Harry Reid when it came to advancing Barack Obama's radical agenda.

Insanity has been defined as doing the same thing over and over again and expecting different results. If true, that means Washington has become a political cuckoo's nest. But it also means we are equally insane if we continue playing the establishment's game. Insanity is curable for those willing to be treated–which leaves Washington out–but to be cured, we must decide to do things differently than we've done them in the past.

A CONVERSATION WITH A FRIEND

About a year before the 2020 election, I wrote an article about a run-in of sorts I had with a former radio colleague, who was once part of a talk radio group known as "The Liberty Lineup," when he insisted that conservatives put aside the Republican Party's betrayal of conservatism and vote "not Democrat" to save America.[316] In a social media post from my friend—we'll call him R.C.—he endorsed Sen. Cory Gardner (R-CO) for no reason other than "#notDemocrat," and I asked him if it wasn't time for "conservatives" in Colorado to stop playing the binary game owned and operated by the duopoly, and to end the practice of voting for the lesser of two evils.

Having completely sold out to Trumpism and the Republican Party, R.C. responded by echoing the talking points we hear every election season from the GOP: "No, David. It's time to hold off the Left a little longer while we organize, grow our ranks, and educate enough people to reclaim our founding principles. In the meantime, grow the hell up."

As I mentioned earlier in this book, conservatives lost their Republican Party home shortly after Ronald Reagan left office, and conservatives were essentially banished once Donald Trump was inaugurated. This gave way to Republicans actively selling us out and bastardizing our values as they broke their promises and then lied about it.

Much like the movie *The Matrix*, R.C. and others like him have made the choice to remain slaves to the system. But the good news is that there are many others who are breaking free of their bondage. For example, former 2016 GOP presidential candidate Carly Fiorina used social media accounts at the time to give her thoughts on how far down the rabbit hole the two-party system had fallen:

In this country, we pledge allegiance to the flag, not the president. We swear fidelity to the Constitution, not the party. Our flag is a symbol of 'one nation... indivisible... with liberty and justice for all.' Our Constitution is the document that protects those liberties and delivers that justice. When we pledge allegiance, we reaffirm our citizenship in a nation founded on ideas and ideals—not ethnicity, race, religion or origin. When we swear to 'protect and defend' the Constitution, we promise to uphold the rights, the laws and the institutions that define and govern our nation.

When did so many Republicans decide that we should also pledge allegiance to The Party and swear fidelity to President Trump? I have been called 'disloyal' because I am critical of Trump. I am not alone. Many others have been intimidated into silence or compelled to defend the indefensible.

It is not a citizen's role to be a 'loyal fan' of one side or the other. We have no obligation to follow party orthodoxy, whatever it is. When we silence our voices, we relinquish our power as citizen leaders to shape the nation. We abdicate our responsibility to help create a 'more perfect union.' And in this country, the citizen, not the President, is sovereign.

Every elected official, including the President, is there to serve the citizenry, not the other way around. **It is not a citizen's job to 'be loyal'; it is the official's job to earn our loyalty. And when they cannot, we vote them out of office**.

As citizens it is both our responsibility and our right to hold elected officials accountable: for their words, their actions and the consequences of both.[317] (Emphasis mine)

At about the same time, Justin Amash (I-MI) sent a tweet pointing out the faux conservatism of the GOP, and he challenged the R.C.s of the world to "walk away" from the GOP and "start something new":

The Republican Party is not a conservative party, and it's not going to be one anytime soon. Conservatives are providing critical votes to a party that actively opposes limited government and free markets. **Walk away, start something new, and regain your voice**.[318]

The hope of "reclaim(ing) our founding principles," as my friend R.C. claimed he was trying to do, remains impossible unless we break free of the Republican/Democrat duopoly. We must, to paraphrase the Scripture found in Hebrews 12:1, "throw off every encumbrance" so that we can "run the race set out before us." The Republican Party is an encumbrance; we need to throw it off so that we can run the race to save America.

THE LESSER OF TWO EVILS

One of my favorite movies is *Master and Commander: The Far Side of the World*, starring Russell Crowe as Captain Jack Aubrey. In one of the lighthearted moments of the movie, Aubrey is having dinner with his officers when he notices two weevils on a plate, and he asks his friend, Dr. Stephen Maturin (played by Paul Bettany) a question:

Aubrey: Do you see those two weevils, Doctor?

Maturin: I do.

Aubrey: Which would you choose?

Maturin: Neither. There's no difference between them. They're the same species of curculio.

Aubrey: If you had to choose. If you were forced to make a choice. If there was no other . . .

Maturin: Well then, if you're going to push me... I would choose the right-hand weevil. It has significant advantage in both length and breadth.

Aubrey: There, I have you! You're completely dished! Do you not know that in the service, one must always choose the lesser of two weevils?[319]

During the 2016 presidential primary, Mitch McConnell was interviewed by Jon-David Wells of the Wells Report. When asked if the general election between Hillary Clinton and Donald Trump was a "lesser of two evils election," Senate Majority Leader Mitch McConnell said on the Wells Report on 660 AM: "Well, it just is. That's an honest answer. This is a choice that many Americans are not happy with. But it is the choice."

We need to abandon the two-party system, a system of the duopoly, by the duopoly, and for the duopoly. We need to refuse to play their game. We need to reject the "lesser of two evils" approach to electing our leaders and decide here and now to *change* the game. Elections have become an abhorrent affair run by abhorrent people, but if we possess the will, we can change that.

EVEN A LITTLE POISON IS DEADLY

Suppose I put two glasses in front of you. The first glass is brimming with a lethal poison. The second one is filled to the top with your favorite beverage mixed with a single drop of the same lethal poison. Which one would you drink from? I'm guessing you wouldn't drink from the first one because it's pure poison. But I bet you would also pass on the second glass because even a little poison is deadly.

For years, when it comes to elections, voters have been told by the duopoly that they need to choose between a full glass of poison (Democrats/Socialists/Marxists) and a glass containing just a little poison in it (Republicans/Nationalists/Fascists). As in the hypothetical example above, neither is really a good idea because they are both deadly to liberty. As conservatives consider the dark future of liberty in America, we need to choose a third glass to drink from. We can no longer settle for the poison being served by both parties.

CHAPTER 19

CHOOSE TO ACCEPT SHORT-TERM PAIN FOR LONG-TERM GAIN

"Those who won our independence... valued liberty as an end and as a means. They believed liberty to be the secret of happiness and courage to be the secret of liberty."[320]

LOUIS D. BRANDEIS

(United States Supreme Court Associate Justice)

"It is only through labor and painful effort, by grim energy and resolute courage, that we move on to better things."[321]

THEODORE ROOSEVELT

(26th president of the United States)

"Do not pray for easy lives. Pray to be stronger men! Do not pray for tasks equal to your powers. Pray for powers equal to your tasks."[322]

JOHN F. KENNEDY

(35th president of the United States)

I n declaring the birth of the United States, Thomas Jefferson drew upon fundamental truths concerning liberty, but he also reminded the world that character and integrity mattered. The most telling example of this was evident in these words from the Declaration of Independence, "for the support of this Declaration, with a firm reliance on the protection of divine Providence, we mutually pledge to each other our Lives, our Fortunes, and our sacred Honor." Quite a commitment, and for many of the fifty-six signers of the Declaration of Independence, it was put to the test. In the days following July 4, 1776, nine of the signers died. They passed before realizing their success, while many of the rest suffered financial losses and, in some cases, total ruin.

Though we may not be required to pay the price our Founding Fathers paid—at least not yet—I think it's safe to say the threat to liberty is the worst it's been in our lifetime, and if things don't change, we could be witnessing the last days of freedom in America. The explosion of liberty-killing big government caused by far-left Democrats and Republican vagabonds devoid of conservative values simply cannot be understated. This is why I'm an equal-opportunity critic of these frauds instead of their cheerleader, because truth is more important than going along to get along, regardless of the short-term pain it may cause.

In the weeks and months following the 2020 election, when the only winner was the Republican/Democrat duopoly, the cost of defending Christian constitutional conservatism was high. I was hammered by friend and foe alike for not bowing my knee to the Washington establishment and for demanding that we reject the two-party system and change the game.

Over recent years, former allies, even those who identify as Christians, have abandoned conservatism and the Constitution—particularly during the COVID-19 "pandemic"—choosing instead to surrender to government tyranny and oppression. When I refused to join them in their surrender, they accused me of violating Romans 13 (the "submit to government authority" Scripture I mentioned earlier) and of not being pro-life because, apparently, refusing to get "the jab" and/or wear a mask was suddenly no different than murdering an unborn child.

In a piece written for BernardGoldberg.com shortly after the 2020 election, commentator John Daly showed us how faux conservatives in the media decided to avoid short-term pain and instead throw their principles, their values, and their dignity overboard for personal gain and a seat at Donald Trump's table:

> Particularly unsettling was watching a number of 2016 election-era **'Never Trump' conservatives**, upon realizing what Trump's White House tenure could mean for their careers, **do a rhetorical about-face on much of what they'd stood and spoken out for over many years**. They even started **publicly attacking their conservative colleagues (including friends), for still saying what they themselves had been saying just months earlier**.

Principles were out. Trump-partisanship was in. And little has changed since then.

Those who chose to maintain their intellectual consistency, personal integrity, and conservative sensibilities paid a significant professional price in the era of Trump—a price that included lost radio shows, less air-time, contributor contracts not being renewed, speaking engagements drying up, and far fewer web-hits.

Those who sold out, by and large, reached new professional heights.

Looking back at that time, it's still pretty striking how easily the political makeover came for some. **People like Mollie Hemingway, Mark Levin, and Greg Gutfeld, who were once outspoken Trump critics, turned into some of the president's most shameless sycophants and defenders.** When one looks back at *National Review's* famous 'Against Trump' issue from 2016, they'll find contributor names like **Glenn Beck, Ben Domenech, Brent Bozell, Katie Pavlich, and Dana Loesch... all of whom now bend over backwards not to say anything the slightest bit disparaging about Trump.** Some are even busy at the moment promoting Trump's 2020 election conspiracy theories.

While it remains unclear if these people will wondrously revert back to their old selves from four or five years ago, **they've already proven that past positions and rhetoric don't particularly matter**... which means it's entirely feasible. Or perhaps they'll just keep saying whatever they think the base wants them to say on any given day. Confirmation bias, after all, is a very powerful thing.[323] (Emphasis mine)

Post-Trump, there was some hope that conservatism would experience a rebound after he was fully exposed as a political opportunist and a fraud. But a conservative Republican Party has been a lost cause ever since John Boehner and Mitch McConnell teamed up to "crush the conservative opposition" in 2014 while simultaneously working hand-in-hand with Harry Reid and Nancy Pelosi to advance the bipartisan socialist/Marxist agenda of the Washington machine.[324]

To see liberty restored in America requires a return to our values. Conservatism remains vitally important, and the need for allies has never been greater. Even though our voices may be drowned out and our efforts mocked and ignored, we must never be silent. We must always speak the truth. Our short-term pain can be a long-term gain if we remain resolute.

In the end, I know we can succeed because our cause is *ALWAYS RIGHT*.

CHAPTER 20

CHOOSE TO GET INVOLVED

"People too smart to get involved in politics are doomed to live in societies run by people who aren't."[325]

PLATO
(Ancient Greek philosopher)

"When a man is denied the right to live the life he believes in, he has no choice but to become an outlaw."[326]

NELSON MANDELA
(Activist, first president of South Africa)

"He who passively accepts evil is as much involved in it as he who helps to perpetrate it. He who accepts evil without protesting against it is really cooperating with it."[327]

MARTIN LUTHER KING, JR.
(Minister, activist, philosopher, leader of the Civil Rights Movement)

"If you see something, say something" became an unofficial catchphrase post-9/11, appearing on billboards and public transportation systems as the government worked to turn citizens into amateur anti-terrorism spies. The Orwellian-sounding mantra was born on Sept. 12, 2001. New Yorker and advertising executive Allen Kay came up with the phrase without a client in mind, but he wanted to create something he believed to be positive in the days after the attack on the Twin Towers. It was eventually adopted by the DHS, the TSA, Amtrak, and cities like Chicago and San Francisco.[328]

This anti-terrorism mantra became Barack Obama's favorite propaganda tool in his feckless attempts to deal with Islamic terrorism, but Donald Trump's DHS left his predecessor in the dust in 2018 when it designated every September 25 as national "If You See Something, Say Something Awareness Day," and they built a website loaded with resources to make better spies of us all.[329]

In February 2021, we learned about a bill that took the see-something, say-something approach to killing liberty and applied it to the government's war on free speech and Big Tech. The See Something, Say Something Online Act was introduced by Sen. Joe Manchin (D-W. Va.) and co-sponsored by Sen. John Cornyn (R-Texas) to take down the federal communications law known as Section 230 and destroy freedom of speech and online privacy.[330] Under this legislation, any interactive computer service provider (social media giants, small blogs, podcast hosting services, app stores, consumer review platforms, independent political forums, and many more) would lose Section 230 protection if they failed to report any known user activity that might be deemed "suspicious." "Suspicious" content is defined as *any* post, private message, comment, tag, transaction, or "any other user-generated content or transmission" that government officials later determine "commits, facilitates, incites, promotes, or otherwise assists the commission of a major crime."[331] Major crimes are defined as anything involving violence, domestic or international terrorism, or a "serious drug offense." For each suspicious post, services would be required to submit a Suspicious Transmission Activity Report (STAR) within thirty days, providing the user's name, location, and other identifying information, as well as any relevant metadata.

Not a good thing for liberty, is it? But what if we fought fire with fire? What if, instead of turning ourselves into de facto spies for the new Axis of Evil, we focused on their tyrannical agenda and then, instead of just "saying something" about it, we did something to change the game?

ACT LOCALLY

Few political races are more important than the election of state legislatures and executives. Republican and Democrat party leaders know that the Constitution severely restricts the federal government's power, which is why they are fighting so hard to destroy that sacred document; it's also why national party leaders focus on state and local elections. Democrats want Democrat-controlled state legislatures and state executives. This provides the party with the ability to carry out the policies they are pushing for on the national level. The same goes for the Republican Party.

This is why the greatest enemy to the new Axis of Evil's thirst for more national power is the local actions of liberty-loving Americans. Our republic was built on the belief in the power of the local government and individual self-governance. Unfortunately, today's American voter tends to focus solely on national elections while ignoring state elections.

Lovers of liberty need to realize that we can't afford to lose the states. Most of the laws, rules, and regulations we live under on a daily basis come from our local governments, not from the federal. Basic logic should motivate us to act locally. Who is your local representative? Do they uphold your state's Constitution? Do they respect the US Constitution? What is their agenda for being in government? This is where we must take the fight.

A PRACTICAL EXAMPLE OF ACTING LOCALLY

Earlier in this book, I mentioned the government's assault on the Second Amendment using so-called "red flag laws." These laws allow local authorities to seize the firearms of citizens without any due process protection. One of the local authorities charged with enforcing these laws is the local sheriff, an elected position.

In 2019, a group of sheriffs in Colorado declared that they wouldn't be enforcing a red flag law passed in the state.[332] Amazingly, but not surprisingly, many in Colorado were dismayed by this decision because, according to them, these sheriffs were putting themselves above the law and essentially committing a crime of their own in the process. In reality, these sheriffs were doing exactly what they're supposed to do under the Constitution; at least that's what the Supreme Court ruled in 1997 when another unconstitutional anti-gun law was attempted.[333]

When the Brady Handgun Violence Protection Act (Brady Bill) was enacted in 1993, sheriffs in several states refused to enforce it and sought to strike it down as unconstitutional.[334] Sheriffs Richard Mack of Graham County, Arizona, and Jay Printz of Ravalli County, Montana, filed a lawsuit (*Printz v. United States*) that reached the Supreme Court. In a 5-4 decision, the Court ruled sheriffs weren't required to enforce the law because it violated the Tenth Amendment.[335] Writing for the majority, Antonin Scalia said the decision was based on the fact that the Founding Fathers created a powerful local government as a check against an oppressive federal and/or state government.[336] Quoting President James Madison, Justice Scalia said:

[T]he local or municipal authorities form distinct and independent portions of the supremacy, no more subject, within their respective spheres, to the general authority than the general authority is subject to them, within its own sphere. (Federalist 39)

Scalia confirmed what the Founders knew about the dangers of an arbitrary, confiscatory, centralized government, and he pointed out how they designed a system of divided power to ensure the checks and balances necessary to protect our liberty.

The office of sheriff is unique in that the holder is directly responsible to the people of the county, not the government or the courts. Sheriffs are elected, not appointed, and they have complete authority to reject the acts of any agency of the government if those acts violate the rights of the people. Remember, the people are where the Founders placed all powers not delegated to the federal government.

There is no lawful authority for judges or a court to direct the law enforcement activities of a county sheriff. He or she is not a part of the judiciary, but holds executive power and can set up a court, impanel a jury, and form a militia or posse to protect the rights of those he represents.

Using words that sound almost prophetic in today's anti-Second Amendment environment, President Madison confirmed that we not only have a right to be armed, but he also confirmed the power of local government to protect us against a tyrannical federal/state government:

> Besides the advantage of being armed, which the Americans possess over the people of almost every other nation, the existence of subordinate governments, to which the people are attached and by which the militia officers are appointed, forms a barrier against the enterprises of ambition, more

insurmountable than any which a simple government of any form can admit of. (Federalist 46)

Your local sheriff is the highest government authority in your county, higher than the governor and even the president of the United States. That means that not only can he or she refuse to enforce red flag laws, but he or she would be negligent in his or her duties to do otherwise.

In the end, the only hope we have of taking back the liberty we've lost is to commit ourselves to act locally in the fight for life, freedom, religious liberty, the *uninfringed* right of every American to keep and bear arms, our founding principles, limited government, fiscal, social, and constitutional conservatism, family values, traditional marriage, and Judeo-Christian values.

Failure to make this commitment will cost us more than we realize.

CHAPTER 21

CHRISTIANS: CHOOSE TO BE MORE SERPENT, LESS DOVE

"If I sit next to a madman as he drives a car into a group of innocent bystanders, I can't, as a Christian, simply wait for the catastrophe, then comfort the wounded and bury the dead. I must try to wrestle the steering wheel out of the hands of the driver."[337]

DIETRICH BONHOEFFER

(Theologian, anti-Nazi revolutionary, founder of the Confessing Church)

"[When] you enter a state of controlled passivity, you relax your grip and accept that even if your declared intention is to justify the ways of God to man, you might end up interesting your readers rather more in Satan."[338]

IAN MCEWAN

(British novelist and screenwriter)

"Stay alert. This is hazardous work I'm assigning you. You're going to be like sheep running through a wolf pack, so don't call attention to yourselves. Be as shrewd as a snake, inoffensive as a dove."

JESUS

(Matthew 10:16 The Message)

My Christian faith and conservative values are often called into question by people who don't exactly see eye to eye with me when it comes to my criticism of the Republican Party. According to these critics, I need to show Republicans more grace—even when caught lying or breaking their promises—because Democrats are much worse. These critics—many of them Republican loyalists or members of the Trump cult—openly accuse me of not being "Christlike" when I point out how:

► Fascist Republicans are no better than socialist Democrats.

► Trumpism and nationalism have destroyed conservatism within the Republican Party.

► Republicans have been sell-outs on abortion for decades.

► "Christian" pro-life groups are no different than 1930s Germany concerning abortion.

► Donald Trump and the Republican Party have embraced the LGBT agenda.

► The Fellowship of the Pharisees has abandoned the Gospel for a seat at Trump's table.

I have no intention of defending myself against these accusers; I have fully documented a myriad of reasons for opposing Democrats, Republicans, and so-called conservatives over the years. Some people may think I am not showing a proper amount of Christian love by doing so, but I disagree. Sometimes speaking truth is the most loving thing one can do.

Fortunately, the measure of my faith and Christlikeness, or lack thereof, is above their pay grade; it's God's call, not theirs. It does, however, cause me to consider exactly what Christian love looks like. Was Jesus showing Christian love when He drove the moneychangers out of the temple with a whip he handmade specifically for that purpose? Was Jesus demonstrating love toward the religious leaders of his day when he referred to them as a "brood of vipers" and chastised them for seeking an escape from the coming judgment? Actually, the answer to these questions is a resounding *yes*! Why? Because love means dealing with things as they are, not only as we wish they were.

When faced with the need to be more serpent and less dove, I'm reminded of a man I mentioned earlier in this book, Dietrich Bonhoeffer. He was the minister Adolf Hitler imprisoned and ultimately hanged for standing in defiance of the evils of Nazi Germany. Bonhoeffer coined a term to describe the social climate of the church in Germany during WWII, which led to her collapse—"cheap grace:"

> Cheap grace means grace as a doctrine, a principle, a system. It means forgiveness of sins proclaimed as a general truth; the love of God taught as the Christian 'conception' of God. An intellectual

assent to that idea is held to be of itself sufficient to secure remission of sins ... In such a Church the world finds a cheap covering for its sins; no contrition is required, still less any real desire to be delivered from sin. Cheap grace therefore amounts to a denial of the living Word of God, in fact, a denial of the Incarnation of the Word of God.

Cheap grace means the justification of sin without the justification of the sinner. Grace alone does everything they say, and so everything can remain as it was before. 'All for sin could not atone.' Well, then, let the Christian live like the rest of the world, let him model himself on the world's standards in every sphere of life, and not presumptuously aspire to live a different life under grace from his old life under sin ...

Cheap grace is the grace we bestow on ourselves. Cheap grace is the preaching of forgiveness without requiring repentance, baptism without church discipline, Communion without confession ... Cheap grace is grace without discipleship, grace without the cross, grace without Jesus Christ, living and incarnate.[339]

I've never been shy about defending my faith and for being a Christian conservative. I've never been shy about pointing out how today's lukewarm cheap grace church has destroyed the Good News of Jesus Christ, creating political conditions similar to those that gave rise to Adolf Hitler and Nazi Germany. Nor have I been shy about the stand I take in defense of my constitutional conservative values and how today's Republican Party and their Democrat counterparts are working hand in hand to destroy liberty.

America has drifted away from the nation envisioned by our Founding Fathers and has replaced liberty with tyranny. Evangelicals have drifted away from the Gospel of Jesus Christ and have replaced it with the cheap grace, lukewarm gospel of progressivism and Christian nationalism.

Fascist. Socialist. Marxist. Nationalist. These are the tyrannical labels of the Republican/Democrat duopoly. Lukewarm. Cheap grace. Compromising. These are the damnable labels of Evangelicals and the Fellowship of the Pharisees. As we witness these destructive trends, we simply cannot stand by and allow this great country to fall under the tyranny of the New Axis of Evil, and we need to reject the passivity and indifference responsible for the destruction of our faith. Taking a stand against these abominations isn't a demonstration of hate, but the ultimate display of love ... for my country and my God.

Jesus instructs Christians to be "wise as serpents and harmless as doves," and as I look at the state of Christian constitutional conservatism in America, today's Christians need to choose to be a little more serpent and a lot less dove. Liberty, the rights of our fellow citizens, their futures, and the future of our great Republic depends on it!

CHAPTER 22

CHOOSE A LITTLE REBELLION

"I hold it that a little rebellion now and then is a good thing, and as necessary in the political world as storms in the physical. Unsuccessful rebellions indeed generally establish the encroachments on the rights of the people which have produced them. An observation of this truth should render honest republican governors so mild in their punishment of rebellions, as not to discourage them too much. It is a medicine necessary for the sound health of government."[340]

THOMAS JEFFERSON

(Founding Father, third president of the United States, author of the Declaration of Independence)

"The only way to deal with an unfree world is to become so absolutely free that your very existence is an act of rebellion."[341]

ALBERT CAMUS

(Philosopher, author, political activist)

"Rebellion to tyrants is obedience to God."[342]

BENJAMIN FRANKLIN

(Founding Father, proposed as the motto for the Great Seal of the United States)

I t was Albert Einstein who has been credited with the quote defining insanity as doing the same thing over and over and expecting different results. While Einstein may or may not have been the originator of the phrase, it has a role to play when it comes to realizing the political change we're going to need to see liberty restored in America.

Under the two-party system owned and operated by Republicans and Democrats for the benefit of Republicans and Democrats, most Americans have been doing the same thing every time the elections roll around. They abandon their consciences to vote for their party's candidate even though the candidate and the party have abandoned the Constitution. In the voters' minds, it becomes more important to vote for the person who toes the party line over the "bad" person representing the other party.

They might be frustrated with how things are going; they might be unhappy with the person representing their party; they might be aware of the threat to liberty and the Constitution. Yet, even when given the opportunity to change the game, they continue putting the same people in office. And even when they vote for someone "different," they merely replace the old representative with an indistinguishable version of the old representative.

We'll never see the political change necessary to save America and return her to conservative values and the Constitution by doing the same thing over and over while expecting different results; it's the literal definition of political insanity.

WHAT IF WE CHOSE TO DO SOMETHING BOLD?

What if we stopped paying attention to political parties, talking points, emotional jargon, and big-name endorsements and started acting like the employers we are? What if we began measuring every candidate against the Constitution at both the state and federal levels? What if we chose to defeat the new Axis of Evil? What if we chose to break free of the Washington Matrix? And what if we chose to work collectively to produce a new kind of candidate (even for smaller local races where the individual running has little or no opposition in his or her race) willing to challenge the party establishment for its failure to protect and defend the Constitution?

Americans have grown comfortable with playing the new Axis of Evil's political game; they pick a few issues they feel strongly about (or issues the parties tell them they should feel strongly about). Republicans declare their version of the "truth," while Democrats declare their version of the "truth." In the end, voters do as the duopoly wishes.

What if instead of simply throwing our hands up and voting the party line regardless of whether or not they know or follow their job description to protect and defend the Constitution, we choose to challenge the party? What if, instead of justifying our continued support of party politics and the candidates who either don't know or don't care about liberty and the Constitution, we choose to hold them accountable and start showing them that we will no longer let them get away with it? What if we risk it all by working for the political change America needs to restore liberty?

POLITICIANS WORK FOR US

It's time to remind politicians at every level of government that they work for us, not the other way around. It's also time to remind "we the people" that we are the employer, not the employee. As employers, we need to know the job description of the men and women we hire to represent us and know if they've been performing their duties satisfactorily; if not, then we need to move away from idle threats and take action.

What if there is a local or national politician representing your party who has voted in favor of legislation that violates the state or national Constitution and is running unopposed? Will you vote for them again simply to keep your party in power? Are you going to be OK with your representatives continually trashing their job description? Are you willing to turn a blind eye because of the *R* or *D* next to their name?

What if we stopped doing the same thing over and over, expecting different results? What if we voted our conscience in favor of a new third party or write-in candidate—one who knows his or her job description and can be a threat to the power brokers of the "shoo-in" party establishment candidate? If the new candidate wins, change can happen. Even if the new candidate loses, change can still happen.

Would the Founding Fathers have succeeded if they simply wrote one letter after another to the king pleading for a respite or change of his policies? If they had done so, they would have been guilty of doing the same thing over and over, hoping for a different result. Instead, they chose to risk everything, declare independence, and challenge the greatest military in the world. Dangerous liberty was worth it. Nothing would have changed otherwise.

Stepping away from blind party loyalty and support is risky, but it's nothing compared to the risks taken by our forefathers. We need to stop simply talking about "taking the risks" for liberty and choose to quit doing the same things we've always done, expecting different results.

It's time for a little rebellion. Liberty is worth it.

ACKNOWLEDGEMENTS

First and foremost, thanks be to God for his calling on my life and for choosing me to be a voice in the wilderness in defense of life, liberty, and the pursuit of happiness.

Thanks to Bill Blankschaen, Jen Truitt, and the army of people at Story Builders who made this book possible. Without their extraordinary guidance and support, this book would still be on the shelves of my mind gathering dust.

Thanks to the army of readers and listeners who regularly encourage me to keep fighting the good fight. I've been tempted many times over the years to abandon my calling when times were rough and retire someplace off-grid to wait out the zombie apocalypse, but your moral and financial support has kept me engaged in the fight.

Finally, thanks to the many friends and family members who know who I am now compared to who I used to be. I am a blessed man.

ENDNOTES

1   Miller, Alice. Thou Shalt Not Be Aware: Society's Betrayal of the Child. New York: Macmillan, 1998.

2   Thoreau, Henry David. "What lies behind us and what lies ahead of us are tiny matters compared to what lives within us." Quoted in BrainyQuote. Accessed April 1, 2024. https://www.brainyquote.com/quotes/henry_david_thoreau_145971

3   Reagan, Ronald. "Inaugural Address, January 20, 1981." Ronald Reagan Presidential Library and Museum. Accessed April 1, 2024. https://www.reaganlibrary.gov/archives/speech/inaugural-address-1981

4   Farmers' Almanac. "5 Foggiest Places in North America." Accessed April 1, 2024. https://www.farmersalmanac.com/5-foggiest-places-north-america

5   World Atlas. "Foggiest Places on Earth." Accessed April 1, 2024. https://www.worldatlas.com/articles/foggiest-places-on-earth.html

6   OnTheIssues.org. "Richard Nixon on Gun Control." Accessed April 1, 2024. https://www.ontheissues.org/Celeb/Richard_Nixon_Gun_Control.htm

7   Vocabulary.com. "Definition of strident." Accessed April 1, 2024. https://www.vocabulary.com/dictionary/strident

8   The Noble Heart. "A Dangerous but Necessary Road." PDF. Accessed April 1, 2024. https://thenobleheart.com/wp-content/uploads/downloads/2010/09/A-dangerous-but-necessary-road1.pdf

9   Ibid

10 Mayo Clinic. "Narcissistic Personality Disorder: Symptoms & Causes." Last modified March 8, 2022. https://www.mayoclinic.org/diseases-conditions/narcissistic-personality-disorder/symptoms-causes/syc-20366662

11 Ibid

12 Ronald Reagan Presidential Library and Museum. "Farewell Address to the Nation, January 11, 1989." Accessed April 1, 2024. https://www.reaganlibrary.gov/archives/speech/farewell-address-nation

13 National Archives. Founders Online. Tully No. III, [28 August 1794].
    Accessed April 5, 2024. https://founders.archives.gov/documents/
    Hamilton/01-17-02-0130

14 National Archives. Founders Online. John Adams to Abigail Adams,
    July 7, 1775. Accessed April 5, 2024. https://founders.archives.gov/
    documents/Adams/04-01-02-0160

15 Henry Clay Estate Ashland. "Henry Clay's Law Career by Justice
    Sandra Day O'Connor." Accessed April 5, 2024. https://henryclay.
    org/henry-clay/the-attorney/henry-clays-law-career-by-justice-
    sandra-day-oconnor/

16 Library of Congress Blogs. "A Republic If You Can Keep It: Elizabeth
    Willing Powel, Benjamin Franklin, and the James McHenry
    Journal." January 6, 2022. Accessed April 5, 2024. https://blogs.loc.
    gov/manuscripts/2022/01/a-republic-if-you-can-keep-it-elizabeth-
    willing-powel-benjamin-franklin-and-the-james-mchenry-journal/

17 Ibid

18 Ibid

19 Orwell, George. 1984. London: Secker & Warburg, 1949.

20 The Strident Conservative. "DHS Misinformation/Disinformation
    Board: Joe Biden's Ministry of Truth." April 29, 2022. Accessed 5, 2024.
    https://www.stridentconservative.com/dhs-misinformation-
    disinformation-board-joe-bidens-ministry-of-truth/

21 The Strident Conservative. "DHS's Ministry of Truth has been
    secretly dismantling free speech." November 7, 2022. Accessed April
    5, 2024. https://www.stridentconservative.com/dhss-ministry-of-
    truth-has-been-secretly-dismantling-free-speech/

22 Wired.com. "Facebook Groups Are Destroying America." June 17, 2020.
    Accessed April 5, 2024. https://www.wired.com/story/facebook-
    groups-are-destroying-america/

23 NPR.org. "Women face disproportionate attacks online. One expert
    shares some of the details." April 16, 2022. Accessed April 5, 2024. https://
    www.npr.org/2022/04/16/1093212502/women-face-disproportionate-
    attacks-online-one-expert-shares-some-of-the-details

24 Reason.com. "Lindsey Graham Wants to Use Mistrust of Big Tech To
    Destroy Your Right to Online Privacy." January 31, 2020. Accessed April
    5, 2024. https://reason.com/2020/01/31/lindsey-graham-wants-to-use-
    mistrust-of-big-tech-to-destroy-your-right-to-online-privacy/

25   Ibid

26   Warren, Elizabeth, and Lindsey Graham. "Warren, Graham
     Unveil Bipartisan Bill to Rein in Big Tech." Press release, July
     27, 2023. Accessed April 5, 2024. https://www.warren.senate.
     gov/newsroom/press-releases/warren-graham-unveil-
     bipartisan-bill-to-rein-in-big-tech#:~:text=The%20bill%20
     would%3A,security%2C%20and%20prevent%20harm%20online

27   The Strident Conservative. "Jesus never taught 'tolerance' - A
     second look after the same-sex marriage ruling." June 29, 2015.
     Accessed April 5, 2024. https://www.stridentconservative.com/
     jesus-never-taught-tolerance-a-second-look-after-the-same-sex-
     marriage-ruling/

28   Folger (Porter), Janet. The Criminalization of Christianity. Published
     February 19, 2009. Penguin Random House.

29   Free Republic. "Chai Feldblum Obama Nominee to EEOC: Gay Sex,
     Polygamy trumps Religious Rights." December 11, 2009.

30   H.R. 5, 116th Cong. (2019), Congress.gov

31   National Review. "Feminist Testifies Against the 'Equality Act'."
     April 2, 2019. Accessed April 5, 2024. https://www.nationalreview.
     com/corner/feminist-julia-beck-testifies-against-equality-act/

32   Nadler, Jerry. "Chairman Nadler's Statement for the Markup
     of H.R. 5, the Equality Act." Press release, May 1, 2019. Accessed
     April 10, 2024. https://nadler.house.gov/news/documentsingle.
     aspx?DocumentID=393904

33   The Strident Conservative. "Republicans offer a 'conservative'
     alternative to pro-LGBT Equality Act." December 11, 2019. Accessed
     April 5, 2024. https://www.stridentconservative.com/republicans-
     offer-a-conservative-alternative-to-pro-lgbt-equality-act/

34   Ibid

35   LifeSiteNews.com. "US Supreme Court votes 6-3 to redefine 'sex,'
     write transgenderism into 1964 law." June 15, 2020. Accessed April 5,
     2024. https://www.lifesitenews.com/news/supreme-court-votes-
     6-3-to-redefine-sex-write-transgenderism-into-1964-law/

36   The Strident Conservative. "Supreme Court same-sex marriage
     ruling will end First Amendment." July 6, 2015. Accessed April 5,
     2024. https://www.stridentconservative.com/supreme-court-
     same-sex-marriage-ruling-will-end-first-amendment/

37 Beito, David T. "FDR's War Against The Press." Reason.com, April 5, 2017. Accessed April 5, 2024. https://reason.com/2017/04/05/roosevelts-war-against-the-pre/

38 Ibid

39 Ibid

40 Ibid

41 Mediaite.com. "Your Move, Media: The Obama Administration Dares The Press To Respond To Intimidation Tactics." May 21, 2013. Accessed April 5, 2024. https://www.mediaite.com/online/your-move-media-the-obama-administration-dares-the-press-to-respond-to-intimidation-tactics/

42 The Strident Conservative. "Joseph Goebbels would love Lindsey Graham." June 5, 2013. Accessed April 5, 2024. https://www.stridentconservative.com/joseph-goebbels-would-love-lindsey-graham/

43 The Weekly Standard. "Shielding What from Whom?" June 3, 2013. Accessed April 5, 2024. https://www.washingtonexaminer.com/magazine/2285849/shielding-what-from-whom/

44 The Strident Conservative. "Trump's DHS to compile data base to spy on journalists, bloggers." April 9, 2018. Accessed April 5, 2024. https://www.stridentconservative.com/trumps-dhs-to-compile-data-base-to-spy-on-journalists-bloggers/

45 The Strident Conservative. "Joseph Goebbels' propaganda principles are paying dividends for Trump." August 8, 2018. Accessed April 5, 2024. https://www.stridentconservative.com/joseph-goebbels-propaganda-principles-are-paying-dividends-for-trump/

46 Business Insider. "Trump tweets the media is 'the enemy of the American People'." February 17, 2017. Accessed April 5, 2024. https://www.businessinsider.com/trump-media-enemy-of-american-people-2017-2

47 Jewish Virtual Library. "Joseph Goebbels: 'The Jews are Guilty!'" November 16, 1941. Accessed April 5, 2024. https://www.jewishvirtuallibrary.org/joseph-goebbels-quot-the-jews-are-guilty-quot

48 Townhall.com. "The Emperor Has No Clue...And His Devotees Couldn't Care Less." February 28, 2016. Accessed April 5, 2024. https://townhall.com/columnists/derekhunter/2016/02/28/the-emperor-has-no-clueand-his-devotees-couldnt-care-less-n2125966

49 The Strident Conservative. "Will Republicans join AOC to create a government-sanctioned news media?" January 14, 2021. Accessed April 5, 2024. https://www.stridentconservative.com/will-republicans-join-aoc-to-create-a-government-sanctioned-news-media/

50 Ibid

51 White House Briefing Room. "FACT SHEET: Biden-Harris Administration Announces Initial Actions to Address the Gun Violence Public Health Epidemic." April 7, 2021. Accessed April 5, 2024. https://www.whitehouse.gov/briefing-room/statements-releases/2021/04/07/fact-sheet-biden-harris-administration-announces-initial-actions-to-address-the-gun-violence-public-health-epidemic/

52 Ibid

53 Gun Owners of America. "GOA Commits to Fighting DOJ's Unlawful Regulation on Pistol Braces." June 7, 2021. Accessed April 5, 2024. https://www.gunowners.org/goa-commits-to-fighting-dojs-unlawful-regulation-on-pistol-braces/

54 White House Briefing Room. "FACT SHEET: Biden-Harris Administration Announces Initial Actions to Address the Gun Violence Public Health Epidemic." April 7, 2021. Accessed April 5, 2024. https://www.whitehouse.gov/briefing-room/statements-releases/2021/04/07/fact-sheet-biden-harris-administration-announces-initial-actions-to-address-the-gun-violence-public-health-epidemic/

55 The Hill.com. "Trump: 'Take the guns first, go through due process second'." February 28, 2018. Accessed April 5, 2024. https://thehill.com/homenews/administration/376097-trump-take-the-guns-first-go-through-due-process-second/

56 The Strident Conservative. "Graham/Blumenthal bill uses mental illness catch-all to seize guns without due process." March 9, 2018. Accessed April 5, 2024. https://www.stridentconservative.com/feds-seize-guns-without-due-process/

57 The Strident Conservative. "The TAPS Act: Sort of like red flag laws on steroids." June 10, 2019. Accessed April 5, 2024. https://www.stridentconservative.com/the-taps-act-sort-of-like-red-flag-laws-on-steroids/

58 ReclaimTheNet.org. "World Bank consultant: 'Digital identity is not enough,' suggests a need for access to data." October 26, 2022. Accessed April 5, 2024. https://reclaimthenet.org/world-bank-digital-identity-access-to-data

59 The Sociable.com. "COVID passport mandates are fueling authoritarian social credit systems, digital identity schemes." August 3, 2021. Accessed April 5, 2024. https://sociable.co/government-and-policy/covid-passport-mandates-authoritarian-social-credit-digital-identity/

60 Horizons. "China Social Credit System Explained - What is it & How Does it Work?" February 11, 2024. Updated. Accessed April 5, 2024. https://joinhorizons.com/china-social-credit-system-explained/

61 ReclaimTheNet.org. "The Digital Dollar Will Not Be Anonymous, Federal Reserve Chair Jerome Powell Says." September 27, 2022. Accessed April 5, 2024. https://reclaimthenet.org/the-digital-dollar-will-not-be-anonymous-federal-reserve-chair-jerome-powell-says

62 Office of Public Affairs, Department of Justice. "Financial Fraud Enforcement Task Force Executive Director Michael J. Bresnick at the Exchequer Club of Washington, D.C." Speech, March 20, 2013. Accessed April 5, 2024. https://www.justice.gov/opa/speech/financial-fraud-enforcement-task-force-executive-director-michael-j-bresnick-exchequer

63 White House Briefing Room. "Fact Sheet: Reauthorization of the Violence Against Women Act (VAWA)." March 16, 2022. Accessed April 5, 2024. https://www.whitehouse.gov/briefing-room/statements-releases/2022/03/16/fact-sheet-reauthorization-of-the-violence-against-women-act-vawa/

64 Boyd, Steven. Letter to Rep. Bob Goodlatte, Chairman of the House Judiciary Committee. August 16, 2017

65 The Strident Conservative. "Is Operation Choke Point making a comeback in GOP-controlled Washington?" March 23, 2018. Accessed April 5, 2024. https://www.stridentconservative.com/is-operation-choke-point-making-a-comeback-in-gop-controlled-washington/

66 The Strident Conservative. "Biden's financial surveillance plan is essentially a PATRIOT Act for the IRS." September 13, 2021. Accessed April 5, 2024. https://www.stridentconservative.com/bidens-financial-surveillance-plan-is-essentially-a-patriot-act-for-the-irs/

67   Supreme Court of the United States. https://www.supremecourt.gov/opinions/21pdf/19-1392_6j37.pdf

68   Goodreads.com. "Quote by Terry Pratchett." Accessed April 5, 2024. https://www.goodreads.com/quotes/412254-if-you-do-not-know-where-you-come-from-then

69   Smith, Margaret Chase. "Declaration of Conscience." Speech delivered to the US Senate, June 1, 1950

70   Federal Reserve Bank of Minneapolis. Interview with Thomas Sowell. September 1, 2001. Accessed April 10, 2024. https://www.minneapolisfed.org/article/2001/interview-with-thomas-sowell

71   Goodreads.com. "Any fool can know. The point is to understand." Accessed April 5, 2024. https://www.goodreads.com/quotes/72361-any-fool-can-know-the-point-is-to-understand

72   Maraniss, David. When Pride Still Mattered: A Life of Vince Lombardi. Simon and Schuster, 1999.

73   Henry, Patrick. "Liberty or Death." Speech given at the Second Virginia Revolutionary Convention meeting at St. John's Church, Richmond, March 23, 1775.

74   Barnhill, John Basil. Barnhill-Tichenor Debate on Socialism. Saint Louis, MO: The National Rip-Saw Pub. Co., 1914.

75   National Archives. Founders Online. "Letter to Abigail Adams, April 26, 1777." Accessed April 10, 2024. https://founders.archives.gov/documents/Adams/04-02-02-0169

76   Shaw, George Bernard. "Maxims for Revolutionists: Liberty and Equality." In Man and Superman, 1903.

77   Paine, Thomas. Common Sense. January 10, 1776.

78   Ibid

79   Ibid

80   Montesquieu. The Spirit of the Laws. 1748.

81   AllAboutHistory.org. "Declaration of Independence and Quotes from the Founders." Accessed April 5, 2024. https://www.allabouthistory.org/declaration-of-independence-and-quotes-from-the-founders-faq.htm

82   Franklin, Benjamin. "Speech To The Constitutional Convention." 1787

83 National Archives. Founders Online. "Letter from John Adams to the Massachusetts Militia, October 11, 1798." Accessed April 10, 2024. https://founders.archives.gov/documents/Adams/99-02-02-3102

84 Jefferson Memorial. Quotations on the Northwest Wall.

85 The Catholic Education Resource Center. "Misquoting Our Founding Fathers." Accessed April 5, 2024. https://www.catholiceducation.org/en/culture/history/misquoting-our-founding-fathers.html

86 Metaxas, Eric. Bonhoeffer: A Biography. HarperCollins, 2012.

87 Ibid

88 Cultural Research Center, Arizona Christian University. "American Worldview Inventory 2020 - At a Glance." March 24, 2020. Accessed April 10, 2024. https://www.arizonachristian.edu/wp-content/uploads/2020/04/CRC-AWVI-2020-Release_01-Worldview-in-America.pdf

89 Ibid

90 Ibid

91 The Strident Conservative. "Global warming and the free market: The Marxist ideology of Pope Francis." October 6, 2020. Accessed April 5, 2024. https://www.stridentconservative.com/global-warming-and-the-free-market-the-marxist-ideology-of-pope-francis/

92 Reason.com. "Inside Ronald Reagan: A Reason Interview." July 1975. Accessed April 10, 2024. https://reason.com/1975/07/01/inside-ronald-reagan/

93 Goldwater, Barry. The Conscience of a Conservative. 1960.

94 BrainyQuote. "Ron Paul Quotes." Accessed April 5, 2024. https://www.brainyquote.com/quotes/ron_paul_411827

95 Scruton, Roger. How to be a Conservative. Bloomsbury Continuum, 2014.

96 National Archives. Founders Online. "Letter to Massachusetts Militia, October 11, 1798." Accessed April 10, 2024. https://founders.archives.gov/documents/Adams/99-02-02-3102

97 Thucydides. History of the Peloponnesian War.

98 Goodreads. "To understand reality is not the same as to know." Accessed April 10, 2024. https://www.goodreads.com/quotes/119146-to-understand-reality-is-not-the-same-as-to-know

99 The Hill. "The Memo: Conservatives change their tune on big government." October 17, 2021. Accessed April 10, 2024. https://thehill.com/homenews/campaign/577021-the-memo-conservatives-change-their-tune-on-big-government/

100 CBS. "Interview with George W. Bush." Conducted on August 21, 1984.

101 George W. Bush White House Archives. "President Promotes Compassionate Conservatism." April 30, 2002. Accessed April 10, 2024. https://georgewbush-whitehouse.archives.gov/news/releases/2002/04/20020430-5.html

102 Conservative Political Action Conference (CPAC). February 12, 2012.

103 Hawley, Josh. "Speech at the National Conservatism Conference." July 18, 2019. Accessed April 5, 2024. https://www.hawley.senate.gov/senator-josh-hawleys-speech-national-conservatism-conference

104 Merriam-Webster.com. "Socialism." Accessed April 5, 2024. https://www.merriam-webster.com/dictionary/socialism

105 Business Insider. "Ron DeSantis Keynote Speech at the National Conservatism Conference." September 11, 2022. Accessed April 10, 2024. https://www.businessinsider.com/desantis-says-republicans-should-copy-him-on-big-business-policy-2022-9

106 Ibid

107 Ibid

108 Goodreads. "Edward Snowden Quotes." Accessed April 5, 2024. https://www.goodreads.com/author/quotes/7140597.Edward_Snowden

109 QuoteFancy. "Michael Badnarik Quote." Accessed April 5, 2024. https://quotefancy.com/quote/1077828/Michael-Badnarik-The-Patriot-Act-is-the-most-egregious-piece-of-legislation-to-ever-leave.

110 Göring, Hermann. Germany Reborn. Elkin Mathews & Marrot LTD., 1934.

111 Bill of Rights Monument Project. "Home." Accessed April 5, 2024. https://billofrightsmonumentproject.org

112 White House Archives. 2002 State of the Union Address. January 29, 2002.

113 Ibid

114 Churchill, Winston. "Speech in the House of Commons." House of Commons, May 2, 1935.

[115] Bush, George W. Interview by CNN. CNN, December 15, 2008.

[116] The Washington Post. "Legal memos released on Bush-era justification for warrantless wiretapping." September 6, 2014. Accessed April 10, 2024. https://www.washingtonpost.com/world/national-security/legal-memos-released-on-bush-era-justification-for-warrantless-wiretapping/2014/09/05/91b86c52-356d-11e4-9e92-0899b306bbea_story.html

[117] Ibid

[118] The Strident Conservative. "Coronavirus hysteria: The end of liberty and the race toward tyranny." March 13, 2020. Accessed April 10, 2024. https://www.stridentconservative.com/coronavirus-hysteria-the-end-of-liberty-and-the-race-toward-tyranny/

[119] The Washington Standard. "This Is A Test: How Will The Constitution Fare During A Nationwide Lockdown?" March 10, 2020.

[120] US Department of Labor, Wage and Hour Division. "Families First Coronavirus Response Act: Employer Paid Leave Requirements." Accessed April 10, 2024. https://www.dol.gov/agencies/whd/pandemic/ffcra-employee-paid-leave

[121] Politico. "Kushner's team seeks national coronavirus surveillance system." April 7, 2020. Accessed April 10, 2024. https://www.politico.com/news/2020/04/07/kushner-coronavirus-surveillance-174165

[122] The Strident Conservative. "Biden and DHS label free speech an act of terrorism." August 16, 2021. Accessed April 10, 2024. https://www.stridentconservative.com/biden-and-dhs-label-free-speech-an-act-of-terrorism/

[123] InspiringQuotes.us. "Donald James quotes." Accessed April 10, 2024. https://www.inspiringquotes.us/author/3851-donald-james.

[124] James Madison, "The Federalist No. 48," in The Federalist Papers, ed. Alexander Hamilton, James Madison, and John Jay

[125] The Matrix. Directed by The Wachowskis. Written by The Wachowskis. Released March 31, 1999.

[126] Rousseau, Jean-Jacques. The Social Contract, Or Principles of Political Right. 1762.

[127] The Matrix. Directed by The Wachowskis. Written by The Wachowskis. Released March 31, 1999.

[128] The Independent. "The Decay of Conscience." December 4, 1873.

129 Goodreads. "Religion today is not transforming people; rather it is being transformed by the people. It is not raising the moral level of society; it is descending to society's own level, and congratulating itself that it has scored a victory because society is smilingly accepting its surrender." Accessed April 10, 2024. https://www.goodreads.com/quotes/902559-religion-today-is-not-transforming-people-rather-it-is-being

130 Chesterton, G.K. Charles Dickens: A Critical Study. New York: Dodd, Mead and Company, 1911.

131 The Washington Post. "Letter to Barack Obama." August 25, 2014.

132 Ibid

133 Ibid

134 The Strident Conservative. "Will Baltimore riots usher in Obama's Gestapo?" May 1, 2015. Accessed April 10, 2024. https://www.stridentconservative.com/will-baltimore-riots-usher-in-obamas-gestapo/

135 Newsbusters.org. "MSNBC's Al Sharpton Calls for DOJ to Take Over Police Across America." May 1, 2015. Accessed April 10, 2024. https://newsbusters.org/blogs/randy-hall/2015/05/01/msnbcs-al-sharpton-calls-doj-take-over-police-across-america

136 The Strident Conservative. "Evangelicals meet with Trump to exchange G-O-D for G-O-P." June 22, 2016. Accessed April 10, 2024. https://www.stridentconservative.com/evangelicals-meet-with-trump-to-exchange-g-o-d-for-g-o-p/

137 Ibid

138 Ibid

139 Inside Edition. "Profane Tape Emerges of Trump Talking About Women: 'Grab Her By The P**'." October 6, 2016. Accessed April 10, 2024. https://www.insideedition.com/19133-profane-tape-emerges-of-trump-talking-about-women-grab-her-by-the-p

140 The Strident Conservative. "Evangelicals defend Trump's sexual assault because 'not Hillary'." October 10, 2016. Accessed April 10, 2024. https://www.stridentconservative.com/evangelicals-defend-trumps-sexual-assault-because-not-hillary/

[141] Huffington Post. "Mike Pence 'Offended' By Donald Trump's Lewd Remarks About Women." October 8, 2016. Accessed April 10, 2024. https://www.huffpost.com/entry/mike-pence-donald-trump_n_5 7f925fce4b068ecb5deef15

[142] Huffington Post. "Top Evangelicals Stand By Trump Despite His Vulgar Comments About Sleeping With Married Woman." October 7, 2016. Accessed April 10, 2024. https://www.huffpost.com/entry/ evangelicals-trump_n_57f83051e4b068ecb5de95fb

[143] Ibid

[144] The Washington Post. "Jerry Falwell Jr. can't imagine Trump 'doing anything that's not good for the country'." January 1, 2019. Accessed April 10, 2024. https://www.washingtonpost.com/lifestyle/ magazine/jerry-falwell-jr-cant-imagine-trump-doing-anything-thats-not-good-for-the-country/2018/12/21/6affc4c4-f19e-11e8-80d0-f7e1948d55f4_story.html

[145] The Strident Conservative. "Ralph Reed: Christians have a 'moral obligation' to vote Trump." October 10, 2019. Accessed April 10, 2024. https://www.stridentconservative.com/ralph-reed-christians-have-a-moral-obligation-to-vote-trump/

[146] The Holy Bible: English Standard Version. ESV. Crossway, 2001.

[147] Reed, Ralph. For God and Country: The Case for Trump. Regnery Publishing, March 2020.

[148] Politico. "'Render to God and Trump': Ralph Reed calls for 2020 obedience to Trump." October 9, 2019. Accessed April 10, 2024. https:// www.politico.com/news/2019/10/09/ralph-reed-trump-book-040920

[149] United States. Congress. House of Representatives. "Articles of Impeachment Against Donald John Trump." December 18, 2019. Accessed April 10, 2024. https://www.congress.gov/116/bills/hres755/ BILLS-116hres755enr.pdf

[150] Washington Watch with Tony Perkins, October 29, 2019

[151] Ibid

[152] Markell, Jan. "Understanding the Times, A World Turned Upside Down." Aired April 4, 2019 and April 11, 2019.

[153] Todd Starnes Show, February 13, 2019

[154] Lou Dobbs Facebook Page. Accessed April 10, 2024. https://fb.watch/ qmu-m4jYrW/

[155] Baptist News Global. "Pro-Trump preachers on message against impeachment probe." November 4, 2019. Accessed April 10, 2024. https://baptistnews.com/article/pro-trump-preachers-on-message-against-impeachment-probe/

[156] Ibid

[157] Bonhoeffer, Dietrich. The Cost of Discipleship. 1937.

[158] Chesterton, G.K. Christendom in Dublin. Sheed & Ward, 1932.

[159] America's Presidents, Knowing the Presidents: George Washington

[160] Colson, Charles. God and Government: An Insider's View on the Boundaries Between Faith and Politics. Zondervan, 2010.

[161] The Sacramento Bee. "Jerry Brown talks religion: Buddhism, Catholicism and listening to mass while working out." January 29, 2023. Accessed April 10, 2024. https://www.sacbee.com/news/politics-government/article271716127.html

[162] Society of Environmental Journalists (SEJ). "Man of Tomorrow: The Relentless Life of Jerry Brown." November 11, 2020. Accessed April 10, 2024. https://www.sej.org/publications/bookshelf/man-tomorrow-relentless-life-jerry-brown

[163] Meet the Press with Chuck Todd, August 6, 2017.

[164] The Strident Conservative. "The Gospel according to Jerry Brown and Nancy Pelosi." December 11, 2017. Accessed April 10, 2024. https://www.stridentconservative.com/the-gospel-according-to-jerry-brown-and-nancy-pelosi/

[165] Ibid

[166] "Governor Brown criticizes President Trump for climate change position as California burns." 60 Minutes, December 8, 2017.

[167] The Strident Conservative. "Bless me father, I'm a global warming denier." April 13, 2015. Accessed April 10, 2024. https://www.stridentconservative.com/bless-me-father-im-a-global-warming-denier/

[168] The Strident Conservative. "Nancy Pelosi says keeping Obamacare is God's will." June 29, 2017. Accessed April 10, 2024. https://www.stridentconservative.com/pelosi-obamacare-gods-will/

[169] Ibid

[170] The Strident Conservative. "Hey, GOP! Planned Parenthood set a baby-killing record in 2019-2020!" February 25, 2021. Accessed April 10, 2024. https://www.stridentconservative.com/hey-gop-planned-parenthood-set-a-baby-killing-record-in-2019-2020/

[171] Lewis, C.S. Mere Christianity. Geoffrey Bles, 1942.

[172] Politico. "Obama's pen-and-phone strategy." January 14, 2014. Accessed April 10, 2024. https://www.politico.com/story/2014/01/obama-state-of-the-union-2014-strategy-102151

[173] Napolitano, Andrew P. "Executive Order Tyranny." Creators.com. February 6, 2014. Accessed April 10, 2024. https://www.creators.com/read/judge-napolitano/02/14/executive-order-tyranny

[174] Twitter. "Tweet by @realDonaldTrump." November 20, 2014. Accessed April 10, 2024. https://twitter.com/realDonaldTrump/status/535441553079431168

[175] USA Today. "'Not leadership': Pence in 2014 criticized using presidential powers on immigration reform." January 10, 2019. Accessed April 10, 2024. https://www.usatoday.com/story/news/politics/2019/01/10/mike-pence-2014-using-presidential-powers-immigration-reform-is-not-leadership/2528793002/

[176] The Strident Conservative. "Executive overreach: Obama's 'pen and phone' has nothing on Trump's." August 4, 2020. Accessed April 10, 2024. https://www.stridentconservative.com/executive-overreach-obamas-pen-and-phone-has-nothing-on-trumps/

[177] Rand, Ayn. Atlas Shrugged. 1957.

[178] Lewis, C.S. God in the Dock: Essays on Theology and Ethics. William B. Eerdmans Publishing Company, 1972.

[179] Myer, John. John Myer: A Collection of his Sermons and Writing, #1. 2016.

[180] Moore, Stephen. "Our Unconstitutional Congress." Imprimis, July 1977.

[181] The Strident Conservative. "Will coronavirus be the pièce de résistance of GOP's socialist agenda?" March 11, 2020. Accessed April 10, 2024. https://www.stridentconservative.com/will-coronavirus-be-the-piece-de-resistance-of-gops-socialist-agenda/

[182] The Strident Conservative. "Trump's coronavirus bailout leaves Bush and Obama in the dust." March 26, 2020. Accessed April 10, 2024. https://www.stridentconservative.com/trumps-coronavirus-bailout-leaves-bush-and-obama-in-the-dust/

183 The Strident Conservative. "Fourth coronavirus stimulus and more big government socialism on the way." April 7, 2020. Accessed April 10, 2024. https://www.stridentconservative.com/fourth-coronavirus-stimulus-and-more-big-government-socialism-on-the-way/

184 The Hill. "Democrats eye major infrastructure component in next coronavirus package." March 30, 2020. Accessed April 10, 2024. https://thehill.com/policy/transportation/490243-democrats-eye-major-infrastructure-component-in-next-coronavirus/

185 The Strident Conservative. "Jared Kushner wants a Patriot Act for healthcare to fight coronavirus." April 9, 2020. Accessed April 10, 2024. https://www.stridentconservative.com/jared-kushner-wants-a-patriot-act-for-healthcare-to-fight-coronavirus

186 Business Insider. "The CDC will set up a coronavirus 'surveillance and data collection system' as part of the $2 trillion stimulus bill, which President Trump just signed into law." March 27, 2020. Accessed April 10, 2024. https://www.businessinsider.com/cdc-coronavirus-surveillance-and-data-collection-stimulus-package-2020-3

187 The Strident Conservative. "Coronavirus tyranny: CDC will use 'vaccination record' cards to track you." December 7, 2020. Accessed April 10, 2024. https://www.stridentconservative.com/coronavirus-tyranny-cdc-will-use-vaccination-record-cards-to-track-you/

188 The Strident Conservative. "New World Order digital COVID-19 vaccine 'passport' being developed." January 18, 2021. Accessed April 10, 2024. https://www.stridentconservative.com/new-world-order-digital-covid-vaccine-passport-being-developed/

189 White House. "Executive Order on Promoting COVID-19 Safety in Domestic and International Travel." January 21, 2021. Accessed April 10, 2024. https://www.whitehouse.gov/briefing-room/presidential-actions/2021/01/21/executive-order-promoting-covid-19-safety-in-domestic-and-international-travel/

190 The Strident Conservative. "Joe Biden, Coronavirus Vaccinations, and the Police State Gestapo." July 9, 2021. Accessed April 10, 2024. https://www.stridentconservative.com/joe-biden-coronavirus-vaccinations-and-the-police-state-gestapo/.

191 CNN New Day, July 7, 2021.

[192] TheHill. "HHS Head: 'Absolutely the Government's Business' to Know People's Vaccine Status." July 8, 2021. Accessed April 10, 2024. https://thehill.com/homenews/administration/562026-hhs-secretary-it-is-absolutely-the-governments-business-to-know/

[193] United States Holocaust Memorial Museum. "THE GESTAPO: OVERVIEW." Accessed April 10, 2024. https://encyclopedia.ushmm.org/content/en/article/gestapo

[194] The Strident Conservative. "CDC spied on millions of Americans during COVID-19 by tracking cellphones." May 5, 2022. Accessed April 10, 2024. https://www.stridentconservative.com/cdc-spied-on-millions-of-americans-during-covid-by-tracking-cellphones/

[195] Vice. "CDC Tracked Millions of Phones to See If Americans Followed COVID-19 Lockdown Orders." May 3, 2022. Accessed April 10, 2024. https://www.vice.com/en/article/m7vymn/cdc-tracked-phones-location-data-curfews

[196] The Strident Conservative. "Coronavirus Hysteria: Remote Learning Tyranny Is Killing Our Children." August 20, 2020. Accessed April 10, 2024. https://www.stridentconservative.com/coronavirus-hysteria-remote-learning-tyranny-is-killing-our-children/

[197] TheCenterSquare.com. "Op-Ed: Pandemic Rules Are Killing Our Kids and Destroying Our Liberties." August 19, 2020. Accessed April 10, 2024. https://www.thecentersquare.com/national/article_4d080062-e21f-11ea-88ce-d3f0fd3187ad.html

[198] KVVU-TV (FOX5–Las Vegas). "CCSD Superintendent Pushes for In-Person Learning Citing Student Suicide Rates."

[199] Ibid

[200] The Strident Conservative. "Coronavirus Christians and the Assault on Religious Liberty." April 6, 2021. Accessed April 10, 2024. https://www.stridentconservative.com/coronavirus-christians-and-the-assault-on-religious-liberty/

[201] The Strident Conservative. "Coronavirus Christians: Reject COVID-19 Vaccinations and You're Not 'Pro-Life'." August 30, 2021. Accessed April 11, 2024. https://www.stridentconservative.com/coronavirus-christians-reject-covid-vaccinations-and-youre-not-pro-life/

202 Reason.com. "Video and Transcript of Justice Alito's Keynote Address to the Federalist Society." The Volokh Conspiracy. November 12, 2020. Accessed April 11, 2024. https://reason.com/volokh/2020/11/12/video-and-transcript-of-justice-alitos-keynote-address-to-the-federalist-society/

203 Ibid

204 Ibid

205 Rebel News. "Pastor kicked Calgary cops from church in viral video: Artur Pawlowski Interview." April 6, 2021. Accessed April 11, 2024. https://www.rebelnews.com/pastor_kicked_calgary_cops_from_church_in_viral_video_artur_pawlowski_interview

206 USA Today. "California Gov. Newsom orders statewide closures, including indoor restaurant operations." July 13, 2020. Accessed April 11, 2024. https://www.usatoday.com/story/news/nation/2020/07/13/california-gov-gavin-newsom-orders-businesses-close-amid-covid-19/5430571002/

207 The Strident Conservative. "Supreme Court shot down California indoor church services ban . . . again." February 9, 2021. Accessed April 11, 2024. https://www.stridentconservative.com/supreme-court-shot-down-california-indoor-church-services-ban-again/

208 Rev.com. "Mayor Bill de Blasio NYC Coronavirus Press Conference Transcript March 27." March 27, 2020. Accessed April 11, 2024. https://www.rev.com/blog/transcripts/mayor-bill-de-blasio-nyc-coronavirus-press-conference-transcript-march-27

209 The Dispatch. "It's Time to Stop Rationalizing and Enabling Evangelical Vaccine Rejection." French Press. August 29, 2021. Accessed April 11, 2024. https://thedispatch.com/newsletter/frenchpress/its-time-to-stop-rationalizing-christian

210 The Strident Conservative. "'Christians' and 'conservatives' are warming up to coronavirus tyranny." March 17, 2021. Accessed April 11, 2024. https://www.stridentconservative.com/christians-and-conservatives-are-warming-up-to-coronavirus-tyranny/

211 Oxford English Dictionary. s.v. "nihilism."

212 National Archives. Founders Online. "Thomas Jefferson letter to Charles Hammond, August 18, 1821."

213 The Federalist Number 47. Edited by John P. Kaminski, Charles H. Schoenleber, and Margaret A. Hogan. Volume 11 of The Papers of James Madison. Charlottesville: University of Virginia Press, 1977.

214 The Strident Conservative. "Pfizer and China developing a digital vaccine passport, social credit system." December 13, 2023. Accessed April 11, 2024. https://www.stridentconservative.com/pfizer-and-china-developing-a-digital-vaccine-passport-social-credit-system/

215 The Strident Conservative. "Pfizer and China developing a digital vaccine passport, social credit system." December 13, 2023. Accessed April 11, 2024. https://www.stridentconservative.com/pfizer-and-china-developing-a-digital-vaccine-passport-social-credit-system/

216 Horizons. "China Social Credit System Explained - What is it & How Does it Work?" February 11, 2024. Updated. Accessed April 5, 2024. https://joinhorizons.com/china-social-credit-system-explained/

217 Ibid

218 The Strident Conservative. "Biden's financial surveillance plan is essentially a PATRIOT Act for the IRS." September 13, 2021. Accessed April 11, 2024. https://www.stridentconservative.com/bidens-financial-surveillance-plan-is-essentially-a-patriot-act-for-the-irs/

219 The Strident Conservative. "Digital currency gives big banks and government control of your money." January 26, 2023. Accessed April 11, 2024. https://www.stridentconservative.com/digital-currency-gives-big-banks-and-government-control-of-your-money/

220 Federal Reserve Bank of Richmond. "Bringing Payments into the Fast Lane." Econ Focus, Third Quarter 2023. Accessed April 11, 2024. https://www.richmondfed.org/publications/research/econ_focus/2023/q3_federal_reserve

221 ReclaimTheNet.org. "The digital dollar will not be anonymous, Federal Reserve chair Jerome Powell says." September 27, 2022. Accessed April 11, 2024. https://reclaimthenet.org/the-digital-dollar-will-not-be-anonymous-federal-reserve-chair-jerome-powell-says

222 The Strident Conservative. "Federal Government Has Been Using the PATRIOT Act to Spy on Us Again." December 10, 2020. Accessed April 11, 2024. https://www.stridentconservative.com/federal-government-has-been-using-the-patriot-act-to-spy-on-us-again/

223 Ibid

224 The Strident Conservative. "Keyword Warrants: Government's Plan to Spy on Your Internet Use." June 9, 2023. Accessed April 11, 2024. https://www.stridentconservative.com/keyword-warrants-governments-secret-plan-to-spy-on-your-internet-use/

225 The Strident Conservative. "'Infrastructure' Bill Provision Lets Government Track Every Trip You Take." August 18, 2021. Accessed April 11, 2024. https://www.stridentconservative.com/infrastructure-bill-provision-lets-government-track-every-trip-you-take/

226 CNBC. "Market Alert Interview." March 26, 2021.

227 Forbes.com. "Biden Administration Reverses Course A Second Time On Per Mile Vehicle Tax." August 8, 2021. Accessed April 11, 2024. https://www.forbes.com/sites/patrickgleason/2021/08/08/biden-administration-reverses-course-a-second-time-on-per-mile-vehicle-tax/?sh=2fdb2a007953

228 The Strident Conservative. "DEA Delivers the Latest Hit to the Constitution." January 27, 2015. Accessed April 11, 2024. https://www.stridentconservative.com/dea-delivers-the-latest-hit-to-the-constitution/.

229 Ibid

230 The Verge. "Exclusive: ICE Is About to Start Tracking License Plates Across the US." January 26, 2018. Accessed April 11, 2024. https://www.theverge.com/2018/1/26/16932350/ice-immigration-customs-license-plate-recognition-contract-vigilant-solutions

231 Congress.gov. "Stay Aware For Everyone (SAFE) Act." April 28, 2021. Accessed April 11, 2024. https://www.congress.gov/bill/117th-congress/senate-bill/

232 CNET.com. "New Bill Could Mandate Driver-Monitoring Systems in Future Cars." April 26, 2021. Accessed April 11, 2024. https://www.cnet.com/roadshow/news/new-bill-mandate-driver-monitoring-systems-future-cars/

233 CarBuzz.com. "Ford, Honda, BMW & GM Join Forces For Radical New ID System." October 20, 2019. Accessed April 11, 2024. https://carbuzz.com/news/ford-honda-bmw-gm-join-forces-for-radical-new-id-system/

234 The Strident Conservative. "Progressives Push for an Executive Order Declaring a 'Climate Emergency'." March 17, 2022. Accessed April 11, 2024. https://www.stridentconservative.com/progressives-push-for-an-executive-order-declaring-a-climate-emergency/

235 The Hill. "Coming Soon: Climate Lockdowns?" February 2, 2022. Accessed April 11, 2024. https://thehill.com/opinion/finance/592011-coming-soon-climate-lockdowns/

236 The Strident Conservative. "Scientists: Pandemic Lockdowns Every
     Two Years Will End Global Warming." March 5, 2021. Accessed
     April 11, 2024. https://www.stridentconservative.com/scientists-
     pandemic-lockdowns-every-two-years-will-end-global-warming/

237 The Washington Examiner. "Gov. Jay Inslee: Democrats Will
     Play by New Rules if Trump's Emergency Declaration Not
     Stopped." February 24, 2019. Accessed April 11, 2024. https://www.
     washingtonexaminer.com/news/2214003/gov-jay-inslee-democrats-
     will-play-by-new-rules-if-trumps-emergency-declaration-not-
     stopped/

238 Ibid

239 The Rachel Maddow Show, MSNBC. "Schumer Calls on President
     Biden to Declare 'Climate Emergency'." January 25, 2021.

240 CNBC. "Sen. Marco Rubio Warns Trump a Border Emergency Could
     Embolden a Future Dem President on Climate Change." January
     9, 2019. Accessed April 11, 2024. https://www.cnbc.com/2019/01/09/
     sen-rubio-trump-declaring-a-national-emergency-over-border-
     security-is-a-slippery-slope.html

241 CNBC. "Sen. Marco Rubio warns Trump a border emergency could
     embolden a future Dem president on climate change." January 9,
     2019. Accessed April 11, 2024. https://www.cnbc.com/2019/01/09/
     sen-rubio-trump-declaring-a-national-emergency-over-border-
     security-is-a-slippery-slope.html

242 New York Daily News. "'We're in a new epidemic': Cuomo issues first-
     in-nation disaster emergency on gun violence in N.Y." July 6, 2021.
     Accessed April 11, 2024. https://www.nydailynews.com/2021/07/06/
     were-in-a-new-epidemic-cuomo-issues-first-in-nation-disaster-
     emergency-on-gun-violence-in-ny/

243 Ibid

244 The Strident Conservative. "Trump's Emergency Declaration: A
     Catalyst for Socialism and Destroying the Republic." February 25,
     2019. Accessed April 11, 2024. https://www.stridentconservative.
     com/trumps-emergency-declaration-a-catalyst-for-socialism-and-
     destroying-the-republic/

245 Twitter. "Tweet by @repcleaver" February 14, 2019, 4:06 PM.
     Accessed April 11, 2024. https://twitter.com/RepCleaver/
     status/1096153825990320129.

246 Lewis, C. S. The Screwtape Letters. Published by Geoffrey Bles, 1942.

247 United States. President (1945-1953 : Truman). "Special Message to Congress on the Internal Security of the United States." August 8, 1950.

248 Reid v. Covert, 354 U.S. 1 (1957)

249 TheBlaze.com. "Judge Napolitano: America Is Becoming 'Dangerously Close to a Police State." December 2, 2014.

250 The Strident Conservative. "Bush, Obama, Trump, Biden: The Founders of America's Police State." November 27, 2023. Accessed April 11, 2024. https://www.stridentconservative.com/bush-obama-trump-biden-founders-of-americas-police-state/

251 Reason.com. "Read Obama's Entire Speech Defending NSA Spying." June 7, 2013. Accessed April 11, 2024. https://reason.com/2013/06/07/read-obamas-entire-speech-defending-nsa/

252 Obama, Barack. "Barack Obama Call to Service." YouTube video, 4:12. Posted by BarackObamadotcom, July 2, 2008. https://www.youtube.com/watch?v=Df2p6867_pw

253 Twitter. "Tweet by @realDonaldTrump." January 25, 2017. Accessed April 11, 2024, https://twitter.com/realDonaldTrump/status/824080766288228352

254 Common Dreams. "'Call It the Surge': Vowing Nationwide Crackdown, Trump Touts Tougher and More Militarized US Police." October 28, 2019. Accessed April 11, 2024. https://www.commondreams.org/news/2019/10/28/call-it-surge-vowing-nationwide-crackdown-trump-touts-tougher-and-more-militarized.

255 Ron Paul Institute. "Patriot Act On Steroids: Trump's Dangerous New 'Pre-Crime' Plan." October 30, 2019. Accessed April 11, 2024. https://ronpaulinstitute.org/patriot-act-on-steroids-trumps-dangerous-new-pre-crime-plan/

256 The Hill. "Trump announces he's sending federal agents to Chicago." July 22, 2020. Accessed April 11, 2024. https://thehill.com/homenews/administration/508566-trump-announces-hes-sending-federal-agents-to-chicago/

257 Pennsylvania Capital-Star. "Former Gov./DHS boss Ridge: 'It'd be a cold day in hell' before he'd let 'uninvited' federal agents into Pa." July 21, 2020. Accessed April 11, 2024. https://penncapital-star.com/civil-rights-social-justice/former-gov-dhs-boss-ridge-itd-be-a-cold-day-in-hell-before-hed-let-uninvited-federal-agents-into-pa/

258 The Hill. "Fox's Napolitano rips 'unconstitutional' Trump crackdown on Portland: 'Just plain wrong'." July 20, 2020. Accessed April 11, 2024. https://thehill.com/homenews/media/508205-foxs-napolitano-rips-unconstitutional-trump-crackdown-on-portland-just-plain/

259 New York Times. "Trump Administration Asks Congress to Reauthorize N.S.A.'s Deactivated Call Records Program." August 15, 2019. Accessed April 11, 2024. https://www.nytimes.com/2019/08/15/us/politics/trump-nsa-call-records-program.html

260 National Security Council. National Strategy for Countering Terrorism. June 2021.

261 Office of the Director of National Intelligence. "Domestic Violent Extremism Poses Heightened Threat in 2021." March 1, 2021. Accessed April 11, 2024. https://www.dni.gov/files/ODNI/documents/assessments/UnclassSummaryofDVEAssessment-17MAR21.pdf

262 Ibid

263 The Hill. "Surgeon general demands data on COVID-19 misinformation from major tech firms." March 3, 2022. Accessed April 11, 2024. https://thehill.com/policy/healthcare/596709-surgeon-general-demands-data-on-covid-19-misinformation-from-major-tech/

264 The Strident Conservative. "DHS Misinformation/Disinformation Board: Joe Biden's Ministry of Truth." April 29, 2022. Accessed April 11, 2024. https://www.stridentconservative.com/dhs-misinformation-disinformation-board-joe-bidens-ministry-of-truth/

265 Office of the Attorney General. "Memorandum for Director, Federal Bureau of Investigation, Director, Executive Office for U.S. Attorneys, Assistant Attorney General, Criminal Division, United States Attorneys." October 4, 2021

266 Washington Free Beacon. "Biden Admin Has Records on Nearly One Billion Gun Sales." January 31, 2022. Accessed April 11, 2024. https://freebeacon.com/guns/biden-admin-has-records-on-nearly-one-billion-gun-sales/

267 ReclaimTheNet.com. "Discover to start tracking gun buyers." February 20, 2023. Accessed April 11, 2024. https://reclaimthenet.org/discover-to-start-tracking-gun-buyers

268 Huxley, Aldous. "The Ultimate Revolution." Speech given at University of California, Berkeley, 1962.

269 Von Mises, Ludwig. Economic Freedom and Interventionism: An Anthology of Articles and Essays. 1990.

270 Dallas Ecumenical Prayer Breakfast, August 23, 1984

271 Andrew Breitbart, "Politics is downstream from culture," QuoteFancy, https://quotefancy.com/quote/1700276/Andrew-Breitbart-Politics-is-downstream-from-culture.

272 The Strident Conservative. "Religious Liberty Lost and Judicial Tyranny Won in Masterpiece Cakeshop Decision." June 5, 2018. Accessed April 11, 2024. https://www.stridentconservative.com/religious-liberty-lost-and-judicial-tyranny-won-in-masterpiece-cakeshop-decision/

273 SUPREME COURT OF THE UNITED STATES. "No. 16-111, Masterpiece Cakeshop, Ltd., et al., Petitioners v. Colorado Civil Rights Commission, et al. On Writ of Certiorari to the Court of Appeals of Colorado." June 4, 2018

274 ChristianToday.com. "Franklin Graham: 'Donald Trump Is A Changed Man. I Trust Him'." November 12, 2016. Accessed April 11, 2024. https://www.christiantoday.com/article/franklin-graham-donald-trump-is-a-changed-man-i-trust-him/100419.htm

275 Newsmax.com. "Franklin Graham: Bakery Ruling 'Huge Win for Religious Freedom'." June 4, 2018. Accessed April 11, 2024. https://www.newsmax.com/newsfront/rev-franklin-graham-scotus-ruling-wedding-cake-gay-couple/2018/06/04/id/864057/

276 Twitter. "Tweet by @RMConservative." June 4, 2018, twitter.com/RMConservative/status/1003643565120028672, twitter.com/RMConservative/status/1003691432769712129

277 American Civil Liberties Union (ACLU). "Press Release: Supreme Court Upholds Basic Principles of Nondiscrimination, Reverses Colorado Civil Rights Commission Decision." June 4, 2018. Accessed April 11, 2024. https://www.aclu.org/press-releases/supreme-court-upholds-basic-principles-nondiscrimination-reverses-colorado-civil

278 Scardina v. Masterpiece Cakeshop, Inc., Colorado Court of Appeals No. 21CA1142, January 26, 2023.

279 The Strident Conservative. "Colorado Christian Baker and Religious Liberty Under Assault … Again." March 25, 2021. Accessed April 11, 2024. https://www.stridentconservative.com/colorado-christian-baker-and-religious-liberty-under-assault-again/

[280] National Review. "A Liberal Law Professor Explains Why the Equality Act Would 'Crush' Religious Dissenters." May 17, 2019. Accessed April 11, 2024. https://www.nationalreview.com/2019/05/law-professor-explains-why-the-equality-act-would-crush-religious-dissenters/

[281] TheWrap.com. "Donald Trump Embraces Gays in Historic Shout-Out at Republican National Convention." July 21, 2016. Accessed April 11, 2024. https://www.thewrap.com/donald-trump-embraces-gays-in-historic-shout-out-at-republican-national-convention/

[282] Politico. "Ivanka Trump and Jared Kushner worked to sink LGBT order." February 3, 2017. Accessed April 11, 2024. https://www.politico.com/story/2017/02/ivanka-trump-jared-kushner-lgbt-order-234617

[283] The Strident Conservative. "Pusillanimous Pence defends Trump's pro-LGBT actions." February 7, 2017. Accessed April 11, 2024. https://www.stridentconservative.com/pusillanimous-pence-considering-a-2024-run-against-treacherous-trump/

[284] National Review. "Don't Ever Forget That Mike Pence Threw Religious Liberty Under the Bus." July 15, 2016. Accessed April 11, 2024. https://www.nationalreview.com/corner/dont-ever-forget-mike-pence-threw-religious-liberty-under-bus/

[285] Politico. "Trump on Buttigieg standing with his husband onstage: 'I think it's good'." May 16, 2019. Accessed April 11, 2024. https://www.politico.com/story/2019/05/16/trump-buttigieg-husband-1329624

[286] The Strident Conservative. "False prophets defend Trump, destroy faith, and demolish America." June 17, 2019. Accessed April 11, 2024. https://www.stridentconservative.com/false-prophets-defend-trump-destroy-faith-and-demolish-america/

[287] Memoirs. Random House Trade Paperbacks, 2003.

[288] Kissinger, Henry. Address to the Bilderberg Organization. May 21, 1992.

[289] Schwab, Klaus. The Fourth Industrial Revolution. Kindle Edition, Crown Currency, 2017.

[290] The American Presidency Project. "George H. W. Bush Address to the Nation Announcing Allied Military Action in the Persian Gulf." Accessed April 9, 2024. https://www.presidency.ucsb.edu/documents/address-the-nation-announcing-allied-military-action-the-persian-gulf

[291] WorldAtlas.com. "What Is The New World Order?" Accessed April 9, 2024. https://www.worldatlas.com/what-is-the-new-world-order.html

292 The Strident Conservative. "Will coronavirus hysteria lead to creation of the New World Order?" April 8, 2020. Accessed April 11, 2024. https://www.stridentconservative.com/will-coronavirus-hysteria-lead-to-passage-of-green-new-deal/

293 Ibid

294 Mises Institute. "From Lockdowns to 'The Great Reset'." August 1, 2020. Accessed April 11, 024. https://mises.org/mises-wire/lockdowns-great-reset

295 World Economic Forum. "The Great Reset: A Global Opening Moment to Turn Crisis into Opportunity." September 21, 2020. Accessed April 11, 2024. https://www.weforum.org/press/2020/09/the-great-reset-a-global-opening-moment-to-turn-crisis-into-opportunity/

296 World Economic Forum. "The Great Reset: A Unique Twin Summit to Begin 2021." June 3, 2020. Accessed April 11, 2024. https://www.weforum.org/press/2020/06/the-great-reset-a-unique-twin-summit-to-begin-2021/

297 The Strident Conservative. "Before Joe Biden, Donald Trump was connected to the Great Reset." February 8, 2023. Accessed April 11, 2024. https://www.stridentconservative.com/before-joe-biden-donald-trump-was-connected-to-the-great-reset-2/

298 Ibid

299 World Economic Forum. "Trump at Davos: Trade, taxes and what America First means for the world." January 26, 2018. Accessed April 11, 2024. https://www.weforum.org/agenda/2018/01/trump-at-davos-trade-tax-cuts-and-america-first/

300 Trump White House Archives. "Remarks by President Trump at the World Economic Forum | Davos, Switzerland." January 21, 2020. Accessed April 11, 2024. https://trumpwhitehouse.archives.gov/briefings-statements/remarks-president-trump-world-economic-forum-davos-switzerland/

301 The Strident Conservative. "Joe Biden and John Kerry advocate global government, the Great Reset." December 9, 2020. Accessed April 11, 2024. https://www.stridentconservative.com/joe-biden-and-john-kerry-advocate-global-government-the-great-reset

302 World Economic Forum. "The Great Reset: Building Future Resilience to Global Risks." November 17, 2020. Accessed April 11, 2024. https://www.weforum.org/agenda/2020/11/the-great-reset-building-future-resilience-to-global-risks/

303 World Economic Forum. "5 levers for decarbonizing the global economy and tackling climate change." January 9, 2023. Accessed April 11, 2024. https://www.weforum.org/agenda/2023/01/five-levers-for-decarbonizing-the-global-economy-davos23/

304 The Strident Conservative. "Joe Biden calls on America to lead in creating 'a New World Order'." March 23, 2022. Accessed April 11, 2024. https://www.stridentconservative.com/joe-biden-calls-on-america-to-lead-in-creating-a-new-world-order/

305 The American Presidency Project. "Address Before a Joint Session of the Congress on the Persian Gulf Crisis and the Federal Budget Deficit." September 11, 1990. Accessed April 11, 2024. https://www.presidency.ucsb.edu/documents/address-before-joint-session-the-congress-the-persian-gulf-crisis-and-the-federal-budget

306 Frost, Robert. "The Road Not Taken."

307 Theodore Roosevelt Center at Dickinson State University. "Theodore Roosevelt Quotes."

308 Goodreads.com. "'Never do anything against conscience even if the state demands.'" Accessed April 9, 2024. https://www.goodreads.com/quotes/229491-never-do-anything-against-conscience-even-if-the-state-demands

309 Thoreau, Henry David. On the Duty of Civil Disobedience. First published January 1, 1849.

310 The Strident Conservative. "Walking the lonely conservative road in the Age of Trump." July 31, 2018. Accessed April 11, 2024. https://www.stridentconservative.com/walking-the-lonely-conservative-road-in-the-age-of-trump/

311 The Matrix Revolutions, 2003, Written and Produced by the Wachowskis

312 Rigmarole Books. Partners in Ecocide: Australia's Complicity in the Uranium Cartel. 1982.

313 Chicago Tribune, September 10, 1978

314 National Archives, Founders Online. "Letter from John Adams to Jonathan Jackson, October 2, 1780." Accessed April 11, 2024, https://founders.archives.gov/documents/Adams/06-10-02-0113

315 Arendt, Hannah. Personal Responsibility Under Dictatorship. 1964.

316 The Strident Conservative. "A conversation with a friend: We must dump the GOP to save America." September 11, 2019. Accessed April 11, 2024. https://www.stridentconservative.com/a-conversation-with-a-friend-we-must-dump-the-gop-to-save-america/.

317 Carly Fiorina Facebook page, September 9, 2019

318 Twitter. "Tweet by @justinamash." September 9, 2019, twitter.com/justinamash/status/1171254713150574594

319 Master and Commander: The Far Side of the World, 2003, Co-written, produced and directed by Peter Weir

320 Whitney v. California (concurring opinion), 1927

321 Skyhorse Publishing, Inc. Theodore Roosevelt on Bravery: Lessons from the Most Courageous Leader of the Twentieth Century. 2015.

322 11th Annual Presidential Prayer Breakfast, February 7, 1963

323 Daly, John. "Where Will Media-Conservatism Go After Trump?" BernardGoldberg.com, December 23, 2020. Accessed April 11, 2024. https://www.bernardgoldberg.com/p/where-will-media-conservatism-go-after-trump

324 The Strident Conservative. "G.O.P. establishment ready to crush the opposition." March 11, 2014. Accessed April 11, 2024. https://www.stridentconservative.com/g-o-p-establishment-ready-to-crush-the-opposition/

325 QuoteMaster.org. "People too smart to get involved in politics are doomed to live in societies run by people who aren't." Accessed April 9, 2024. https://www.quotemaster.org/qa341b0ba17d08acfa1e1dae21697d824

326 Pan Macmillan. Nelson Mandela By Himself: The Authorised Book of Quotations. 2011.

327 Plume. The Wisdom of Martin Luther King, Jr. 1993.

328 Department of Homeland Security. "If You See Something, Say Something®." Accessed April 9, 2024. https://www.dhs.gov/see-something-say-something/about-campaign

329 Department of Homeland Security. "If You See Something, Say Something® #SeeSayDay." Accessed April 9, 2024. https://www.dhs.gov/see-something-say-something/seesay-day.

330 The Strident Conservative. "'See Something, Say Something Online Act' equips state to spy on us." February 3, 2021. Accessed April 11, 2024. https://www.stridentconservative.com/see-something-say-something-online-act-equips-state-to-spy-on-us/

331 Ibid

332 CBS News, 60 Minutes. "Several Colorado sheriffs say they won't enforce red flag gun law." November 15, 2019.

333 The Strident Conservative. "Sheriffs have constitutional power and duty not to enforce red flag laws." November 25, 2019. Accessed April 11, 2024. https://www.stridentconservative.com/sheriffs-have-constitutional-power-and-duty-not-to-enforce-red-flag-laws/

334 Thoughtco.com. "The Brady Bill and Background Checks for Gun Buyers." Updated February 2, 2022. Accessed April 11, 2024. https://www.thoughtco.com/brady-act-gun-buyer-background-checks-3321492

335 Printz v. United States, 521 U.S. 898 (1997)

336 Ibid

337 Christianity.com. "Bonhoeffer Executed on Hitler's Order." Updated January 17, 2022. Accessed April 11, 2024. https://www.christianity.com/church/church-history/timeline/1901-2000/bonhoeffer-executed-on-hitlers-order-11630781.html

338 BrainyQuote. "Ian McEwan Quotes." Accessed April 9, 2024. https://www.brainyquote.com/authors/ian-mcewan-quotes

339 Bonhoeffer, Dietrich. The Cost of Discipleship. Originally published in 1937. Revised edition, Collier Books, 1963.

340 National Archives. Founders Online. "Letter from Thomas Jefferson to James Madison, January 30, 1787." Accessed April 11, 2024, https://founders.archives.gov/documents/Jefferson/01-11-02-0095

341 Vintage Books. The Rebel: An Essay on Man in Revolt. 1956.

342 National Archives. Founders Online. "Proposal for the Great Seal of the United States." Before August 14, 1776. Accessed April 11, 2024. https://founders.archives.gov/documents/Franklin/01-22-02-0330